W9-AES-658

THE MEANING OF TRADITION

ABOUT THE BOOK

Although considerable areas of disagreement remain, the long antagonistic Catholic and Protestant views on the relation of scripture and tradition have grown more and more closer. Within the Catholic community one of the leading forces behind this ecumenical rapprochement has been Josef Rupert Geiselmann of the University of Tübingen. In the present book Geiselmann shows that in the earliest period of Christianity it was by tradition that God's revelation in Christ was communicated and handed down. While this tradition was unique, as a religious phenomenon its roots went back to the common tradition first evident in primitive man and expressed in its purest state in the divinely sanctioned tradition of the chosen people. It is one of the major achievements of his treatment of this subject that Geiselmann re-establishes the orthodoxy of many of the underlying insights of de Lamennais, particularly as these were incorporated into the teachings of the *école romantique* of Tübingen. In the last part of this study the author discusses the nature of religious tradition as a universal human reality which attains its highest perfection in the Judaeo-Christian tradition.

QUAESTIONES DISPUTATAE

JOSEF RUPERT GEISELMANN

THE MEANING OF TRADITION

75121

BT
90
. G31

BTQ 253 .G31   ST. JOSEPH'S UNIVERSITY   STX
The meaning of tradition.

3 9353 00007 1512

HERDER AND HERDER

1966

HERDER AND HERDER NEW YORK

232 Madison Avenue, New York, N.Y. 10016

Original edition, the first three chapters of
"Die Heilige Schrift und die Tradition",
Herder, Freiburg, 1962
Translated by W. J. O'Hara

Nihil Obstat: Joannes M. B. Barton, S.T.D., L.S.S.
Censor deputatus

Imprimatur: ✠Patritius Casey, Vic. Gen.
Westmonasterii, die 17° Januarii, 1966

The Nihil Obstat and Imprimatur are a declaration that a book
or pamphlet is considered to be free from doctrinal or moral error.
It is not implied that those who have granted the Nihil Obstat and Imprimatur
agree with the contents, opinions or statements expressed.

Library of Congress Catalog Card Number: 66-10597
First published in West Germany © 1966 Herder KG
Printed in the Republic of Ireland by Cahill & Co., Ltd.

CONTENTS

I

TRADITION IN CHRISTIANITY

1. *The nature of paradosis*

According to the New Testament, paradosis is the form in which the Gospel of Jesus Christ comes to us (Jude 3). The second Letter of Peter (2:20) assumes that knowledge of our salvation in Jesus Christ is conveyed to us by paradosis. It has its source in the testimony of the Twelve, and the content of their paradosis is their witness to Jesus' sufferings, death and resurrection as saving events; in other words, the sacred history of redemption which is concluded by the ascension. Ultimately the paradosis is based on the fact that the history of redemption is concluded.

This closed character was not at all such a matter of course as some may think today. In the early Church people might have believed that the Lord must appear to his own as often as his advice and help proved necessary. That would have been a possible interpretation of his saying " And lo, I am with you always, to the close of the age " (Mt 28:20). Even in the early Church there could have been people who, like Simeon the New Theologian later, held the belief that each generation needs its own leader, and who might have claimed to have seen the glory of the Lord just as Paul had (cf. to some extent Swedenborg). If they had been right there could have been no question of paradosis being the only form in which the saving message of Jesus Christ comes to us. But according to the faith of the primitive Church that was not the case. The existence of that Church was determined by the fact that the day of the Lord's ascension marked the end of the time when he went in and out among us.[1] From then on the situation of the Church is constituted by the fact that " heaven must receive (Jesus Christ) until the time for establishing all that God spoke by the mouth of his holy prophets of old " (Acts 3 : 21). That indicates clearly that what took place on earth in Jesus is concluded and belongs to the past.[2] Henceforth, therefore, these events can only be known as history in general is known, by way of testimony (*martyria*), that is to say, by tradition. The mode of tradition, however, is determined by the nature of what has to be handed on, and as the events connected with the name of Jesus are not historical events of the usual kind, but God's saving and redeeming action, the paradosis cannot simply be of the same kind as the tradition by which ordinary historical events come down to us.

The paradosis is report and kerygma, not a mere report concerning the historical Jesus, as the liberal theology of the end of the nineteenth and beginning of the twentieth century maintained. Neither, however, is it merely kerygma regarding Jesus, as Bultmann would have it. It is report and kerygma, or better still, report in the form of kerygma, a report of what happened in Jesus Christ, and kerygma, proclamation of the joyful message of salvation which has been realized in these historical events and which is made present again and again in the kerygma, so that we are summoned to " hear " and to believe. This confronts us with the remarkable paradox that this kerygma unites in itself the then and the now: the " then " that happened and is past, and the " now " in which that happening is made present. But this " now " does not simply signify the empirical instant in the ordinary sense, lying between past and future, the moment of *chronos*, but also the " now " which God has brought about, the *kairos*, that is to say, the moment of grace given to me by God, which comes upon me and places me before a decision for or against, and in this way decides my future, the *eschaton* which includes the future: " Now is the day of salvation " (2 Cor 6:2). That is the reason why the conception of the history of Jesus contained in the paradosis is " an understanding of history based on the End and in view of the End ".[3] The kerygma in its original apostolic form shows this. The apostles announced Jesus as the Christ by taking as the starting point of their proclamation Old Testament prophecy and interpreting this as fulfilled in Jesus Christ in the light of the events of Easter and Pentecost, that is, on the basis of the End. But the apostolic kerygma does not do this simply in relation to the Old Testament. The words once spoken by Jesus, and the events of his life, were also submitted in the apostolic preaching to an interpretation based on the End, that is to say, on the Easter event. Consequently the paradosis does not reproduce the " then " that happened with historiographical detail but in the form of what is now present, that is to say, in its historical significance. In fact one may even say that precision of historical detail would destroy the paradoxical unity of then and now, in favour of the " then ". Consequently the paradosis cannot really reproduce what Jesus once said " literally ", because it is intended to be Jesus' word now, in the Church's situation as God has brought it about. That is the reason for the two apparently contradictory marks of tradition, on the one hand its incontrovertible fidelity and attachment to Jesus' words and on the other the astonishing degree of freedom regarding their literal historical tenor.[4]

If we seek the reason for this astonishing liberty, it clearly cannot lie in human caprice. The question in fact reveals a new feature of the paradosis. The Church can only allow itself so surprising a degree of freedom in its paradosis of Jesus' words, because that freedom is based on and supported by the operation of the Holy Spirit within the domain of the Church and therefore in the paradosis itself. And that freedom was not only practised by the Church of the apostles but continued in the ecclesiastical tradition of the post-apostolic period, which of course had the task of preserving the *paratheke* (1 Tim 6:20). That safe-keeping could not consist " in mechanical reproduction and transmission of a tradition that had not been understood and which soon became unintelligible ".[5] On the contrary, when Gnosis with its false view of the paradosis invaded the Church, the new situation demanded a correct understanding and paradosis became doctrine as well. That took place even in the apostolic paradosis, as for example when Paul (1 Cor 15:3-5) reproduces the paradosis which he had received from the Twelve and does it in such a way that he at the same time interprets it. This shows that the " now ", the perpetually rendering present of Jesus' words in the Church's paradosis, requires an intelligent reception and transmission of apostolic tradition, behind which there stands the operation of the Holy Spirit who makes a tradition a living doctrinal substance which is to be preserved from falsification and distintegration and subjected to an historical process of ever more profound understanding within the Church. Kerygma in the form of ecclesiastical tradition is always an interpretation of Jesus' words in view of the End, that is to say, from the point of view of here and now, the present situation. For only in that way are the words that Jesus once spoke, his Word here and now.

The Gospel in the form of paradosis and more particularly in the form of interpretative apostolic paradosis remains, however, from first to last the Gospel announced by Jesus (*evangelium a Jesu Christo promulgatum*, cf. Council of Trent, Session 4; Denzinger 783), Jesus' word and the word of God, for by assuming the form of paradosis, the fact that it was received from the Lord (1 Cor 11:23), is not affected. " It is of course to be preserved as such and that means, not supplemented or altered, but understood, expounded, and handed on; it is to be explained and unfolded as the same apostolic Gospel and apostolic bequest. But from first to last, since the Gospel even in the form of Tradition remains the Word of God in the mouths of the apostles and unfolded by the power of the Holy Spirit, it continues to be preserved ' through the Holy Spirit who dwells within us ' (2 Tim 1:14) and is understood and expounded precisely as that Gospel. The Gospel as the Word of God in the mouths of men not only did not lose its nature by its transmission to the Church in the hands of the apostles and their followers; only then did it attain the full expression of its nature." [6]

Paradosis, therefore, is the form in which the Gospel is pro-

13

claimed within the sphere of the Church. The Church owes its existence to God's action in Jesus Christ for the salvation of the world. Consequently, paradosis is the norm of preaching corresponding to the Church's nature. The New Testament itself bears witness to this. The Gospel is the Word, conveyed by tradition. That has been clearly stated in recent times by R. Bultmann, a witness who certainly cannot be suspected of partiality, when in opposition to R. Sohm, he found himself obliged to observe: " Sohm imagines the members of the Christian communities one-sidedly, as religious individualists and enthusiasts, and regards the operation of the Spirit one-sidedly, as taking place in momentary inspirations. He regards as normal as it were what Paul (1 Cor 12 and 14) opposed as a danger or at least restricted. However much momentary inspiration may determine the speech of those endowed with charismatic gifts, the word which they speak does not derive its content from a revelation conceded to them personally by internal enlightenment. They proclaim the ' word of faith ' (Rom 10:8), the *evangelium,* in the centre of which stands Christ and the saving event, the ' word of the cross ' (1 Cor 1:19), ' the message of reconciliation ' (2 Cor 5:20). In however richly varied a form that may occur, as of course the New Testament shows, it is a definite word, conveyed by tradition, and there has never been an *evangelium* without *paradosis* (1 Cor 15:1f.)." [7] And there is a reason for this. " As the community is not founded by the persons who comprise it as an association or fraternity, but knows that it is founded by God's action, it needs, like the Jewish community of the Old Testament, the tradition in which the history on which it is founded is contained and rendered present." [8] The kerygma in the form of the Church's paradosis is, therefore, never directly addressed to an individual as an individual, but to the community as a whole and to the individual as a member of the community. With this we are in possession of the necessary presuppositions for raising the question of the constitutive features of tradition.

2. *External tradition in the form of martyria*

As tradition concerns the events of redemptive history connected with the name of Jesus, paradosis in form is equivalent to proclamation by *martyria*, that is, by bearing witness to these events. This witness testifies to faith in salvation in Jesus Christ and it is testimony which derives from faith in him. It is therefore possible to say who has to bear this witness. It can only be all members of the community of faith, that is, the whole Church, if not all in the same way. Within this *martyria* there are value differences and a hierarchy can be distinguished in the giving of testimony. But it is not the fact of bearing witness which can serve as a criterion to distinguish within the community as a whole some who testify and others who simply receive it. It is true that pre-eminence belongs to the testimony of the apostolic office, the episcopate and the primacy, that is to say, to testimony which derives from mission and apostolic office. That of course is authentic and in certain conditions authoritative testimony; at all events it is public testimony. As, however, what is pre-eminent inevitably attracts attention, there is always a danger of attributing absolute value to it and of seeing tradition purely and simply in the testimony of the magisterium (Dieckmann, A. Deneffe). This line, if carried further, would logically lead in the end to identifying tradition with the testimony of the Roman primate alone, and so provide a dogmatic foundation and justification for the words alleged to have been spoken on the 19th June 1870 by Pius IX, " I am Tradition ".[9] The testimony of the magisterium in all its forms is ecclesiastically authentic and, when given by a general council or by a doctrinal decision *ex cathedra* by the pope, it is the authoritative testimony to apostolic paradosis in the Church. But this magisterium itself, by the way in which it gives its authentic testimony, is opposed to any equating of the pronouncements of the magisterium with tradition. After all, the Fathers of the Council of Trent repeatedly referred to Tradition in their pronouncements [10] and the proclamation by Pius IX and Pius XII of the two dogmas of Mary's Immaculate Conception and Assumption into heavenly glory only took place after the testimony of the bishops, priests and faithful regarding them had been gathered and in that way the Church's paradosis ascertained by the witness of the whole Church. The introduction of the feast *Beatae Mariae Virginis Reginae* is based, in Pius XII's encyclical of the 18th November 1954, *Ad caeli Reginam,* " ex christianae vetustatis monumentis, ex liturgicis precibus, ex indito christiano populo religionis sensu, ex operis arte confectis ".[11] Here, therefore, appeal was made to the Christian people endowed with a religious " sense " as a witness to tradition. So all members of the Church's community, both those who announce and those who hear, are recognized as witnesses to tradition, and since they are all believers, that means the community of the faithful in general.

But what is the nature of this ecclesiastical testimony, and consequently of the Church's tradition? The transmission of the paradosis to the Church by the apostles took place *Spiritu Sancto dictante* (Denzinger 783). The apostles were therefore organs of the Holy Spirit; the transmission was a divine action. The committing to writing of the apostolic paradosis also took place *Spiritu Sancto inspirante,* so that the Holy Spirit is, if not the actual composer, nevertheless by means of the sacred writers, the author of holy Scripture. In contrast to this, the testimony of ecclesiastical tradition is a human action. But that does not mean it is a purely human matter, for behind this human action stands the mission from Christ in which the mission of the Son by the Father is continued, and behind it there also stands the operation of the Holy Spirit in the Church's domain. It is the *certum charisma veritatis,* when apostolic tradition is in question.[12] And it seems to me that this charisma is far from being exhausted by the mere " assistance " of the Holy Spirit and preservation from error thereby, the *assistentia mere negativa.* It comprises the various gifts of the Holy Spirit when the faithful are in question; for these gifts were not restricted to the early Church. The Spirit continues to blow where it wills. The prophetic office continues in the Church. At all events it is a matter of men endowed by the Holy Spirit when the testimony of the faithful to apostolic tradition is in question, for their witness is given out of faith and love, in the Holy Spirit. That is its ground when the faithful take an active part in ecclesiastical tradition. Their testimony is a relatively independent witness, produced by the Holy Spirit, to the truth in Christ entrusted to the Church in the apostolic deposit of faith. That is why Paulinus of Nola admonishes us: " Ab omnium fidelium pendeamus, quia in omnem fidelem Spiritus Sanctus spirat " (*Epistula* 4).

This testimony is of a special kind and by the nature of the case is different from the testimony of those who are entrusted with the preaching of the Gospel. It is not an authentic, and still less an authoritative, testimony, not an official, public testimony at all. But it becomes public testimony when the faithful, as members of the community at divine worship, make the liturgical confession of faith, when they actively join in performing the liturgy of the Church. John Michael Sailer saw in the solemn public worship of God " in accordance with its original dignity, as it were a living propagation of religion in the world around and a living transmission of religion to posterity ".[13] And if for Sailer the Apostles' Creed was the essence of apostolic tradition in words, the Sundays and feast days of the Lord were " a living creed and carry the confession of faith from mouth to mouth to posterity ".[14] In this living participation in the Church's life of divine worship, the faithful in union with the faithful of the whole Church bear public witness to their belief, as they also do in the various forms of divine service which vary from diocese to diocese,[15] each with its own prayer-books and hymn-books, and in the special feasts proper to each locality (patron saints, feast of the dedication of a church), in their special hymns and prayers and special customs for Advent, Christmas, Passiontide and Easter, in the various local pilgrimages which are often determined by ancestry, as, for instance, the pilgrimage to Maria Einsiedeln is a favourite of the Alemanni, a last remaining expression of what was once the unity of their nation—an ethnological testimony to the faith.

18

The witness borne to the faith by the faithful finds eminent expression, however, in the practical life of faith which animates their families. The family of course is the sociological reality which to an exceptional degree is the guardian of tradition. But besides this, there is the private testimony of the individual believer in his confession of the faith in the fidelity of a life in conformity with faith, a *martyria* which in certain circumstances can lead to martyrdom. What Maurice Blondel so pertinently says regarding the nature of tradition is particularly true of this testimony borne by the faithful; " Garder la parole de Dieu, c'est d'abord la pratiquer; et le dépôt de la Tradition que les infidelités de la mémoire et les étroitesses de l'intelligence déformeraient inévitablement, s'il nous était livré sous une forme tout intellectuelle, ne peut être transmis, bien plus, ne peut être employé et développé, que s'il est confié à l'obéissance pratique de l'amour. L'action fidèle est l'arche d'alliance, où demeurent les confidences de Dieu, le tabernacle, où il perpétue sa présence et ses enseignements."[16] But the witness borne by the faithful is only the external expression of an inner testimony which corresponds to a special attitude of mind on their part.

3. Interior tradition. The sensus fidelium

Melchior Cano (*De Locis theologicis,* IV, 1) and with him the Spanish theologians Valencia, Suarez, Ripalda, de Lugo speak of the *sensus fidelium*.[17] Möhler sees the source of the testimony of the faithful in a special Christian tact or flair, a deep and sure feeling which guides and directs into all truth, a deep inner sense.[18] In his French translation of Möhler's *Symbolik*, Lachat renders Möhler's word "tact" by "instinct".[19] Newman then took the word "instinct" from this translation and described this attitude of mind as a kind of instinct.[20] Pius XII's encyclical *Ad coeli Reginam* (18 November 1954) speaks of the *inditus christiano populo religionis sensus,* the special religious "sense" with which the Christian people is endowed.[21]

It would be just as mistaken, however, to regard this "sixth sense", as it were, that the faithful possess through the faith and love produced in them by the spirit as an irrational feeling without object, as it would be to give it independent status, isolating it from the enduring testimony of the successors of the apostles in the Church. The "sense" always remains linked to the witness borne by the apostolic ministry and is an organic part of the testimony of the Church as a whole. Möhler indicates this inner link when he describes this special Christian tact as a sure, profound feeling which leads to all truth, a profound inner sense which alone is adapted to hearing and assimilating the Word of God. For this religious sense of the faith to accrue to the Christian people there is necessary not only the higher life-giving principle of the Holy Spirit, his grace and light of faith and his love infused into men's hearts, but also a trustful adherence to the apostolic ministry which endures in the Church, as well as education in the Church, a hearing, learning and above all a living in it and with it. In that way the sense of faith becomes a sense of the Church, the *sensus fidelium* becomes the *sensus ecclesiasticus.* On account of the connection between tradition and Scripture, however, this *sensus ecclesiasticus* forms, according to Möhler, a special *sensus* in regard to holy Scripture,[22] an "instinct scripturaire".[23] Only this fully comprises what we have to understand by this special Christian tact or flair. As, however, those men, to whom the office of preaching the Gospel has been entrusted, are themselves believers even apart from their ministry, they too enjoy the same higher vital principle of the Holy Spirit which animates the faithful, his grace and light of faith and his love infused into their hearts, from which this spontaneous unreflecting attitude, the *sensus fidelium,* springs. In this way the *christianus populus* comprises all members of the Church and makes of the latter a society of those who believe. This *sensus fidelium, sensus ecclesiasticus* or *inditus christiano populo religionis sensus*, therefore, belongs to all equally, to those who announce the Gospel inasmuch as they are believers, as well as to their hearers.[24] That is the reason that justifies Möhler in equating this *sensus ecclesiasticus* with tradition in the subjective sense. For tradition for him is " the special sense present in the Church and perpetuated through the Church's transmission, which, however, is not to be thought of without its content, for it takes form from its content and through its content, so that it may be called a sense actually functioning. Tradition is the word perpetually living in the hearts of the faithful . . . This awareness of the Church is tradition in the subjective meaning of the word."[25]

This sense is described and defined throughout, however, as something inward and interior. But tradition signifies bearing witness to the apostolic paradosis. Consequently this special tact of the Christian people can only become a witness to apostolic tradition if it finds external expression. This happens in the first place in the instinctive, unreflecting reaction against anything that is not in accordance with the apostolic paradosis. But the function of the *sensus fidelium* as a form of the Church's tradition is not exhausted by this negative reaction. In the past it has also made a positive contribution to the continually advancing understanding of the apostolic paradosis and will continue to do so.[26] The *inditus christiano populo religionis sensus* contributed its share to the increasing understanding of the apostolic paradosis concerning the Mother of the Lord from the Council of Ephesus in 431 down to 1 November 1950 : the dogmas of Mary the *theotokos,* immaculately conceived, assumed into heavenly glory; the belief (not yet raised to a formal dogma) in Mary the Queen of Heaven which by a special feast has been incorporated into the liturgy of the Church and so is solemnly confessed by the *ecclesia orans*—all these were supported and maintained by the *sensus ecclesiasticus* of the faithful before there was any question of the proclamation of a dogma or the institution of a feast in the liturgy of the Church.[27] The same is true of devotion to the Sacred Heart and of the introduction of a feast of the Sacred Heart. This sense of the faith among the people can even stand contrary to a teaching authority in the Church, as the Arian disturbances showed, and as became clear in the opposition of the people to the sermons of Pope John XXII and the General of the Franciscans, Gerard Eudes, in the question of the beatific vision following death immediately in the case of perfectly purified souls. The energetic opposition of the Christian people's sense of the faith was roused against the opinion of the pope that the vision of God was postponed until the Last Day. Hence the petition of the University of Paris that the pope might " confirm by apostolic decision the belief of the whole Christian people entrusted to his guidance which until now had prompted their devoted respect ".[28] The sense of the faith is capable of divining with the logic of a believing heart what cannot be grasped by the reason of mere reasoners or experts.[29] For it is true of the faithful and of the Church that " Sa mémoire du Christ est la mémoire du coeur, non une pure mémoire intellectuelle."[30]

4. *The apostolic paratheke and the Church's tradition*

Through the transmission of the apostolic paradosis to the Church under the double form of living kerygma and its written expression in Scripture (cf. 1 Tim 6:20; 2 Tim 1:12 and 14; 2 Tim 3:15), it becomes the paratheke, the apostolic bequest which is committed to the Church's safe-keeping. By the fact, however, that Scripture and tradition are combined in the idea of the paratheke, it is immediately clear that the two are related by mutual dependence and Möhler's observation is confirmed that, " Church, Gospel and tradition always stand and fall together." [31]

If it is true that " there has never been a Gospel without paradosis ",[32] it is equally the case that there was never an apostolic kerygma without Scripture. There was no apostolic preaching in isolation from Scripture and consequently no apostolic paradosis completely divorced from Scripture. Philip preached the Gospel of Jesus by taking Isaias 53:7 as a basis (Acts 8:26-38), and according to Paul the proclamation of the saving events of Jesus' death and resurrection takes place " according to the scriptures " (1 Cor 15:3-5). Philip's kerygma

and the paradosis reported by Paul, however, may be taken
as typical of apostolic preaching and paradosis generally. And
from the fact that both paradosis and Scripture are entrusted
as a paratheke to the Church's safe-keeping,[33] we may conclude
that they do not stand opposed as two completely separate
realities, but are complementary and mutually related. This is
already clear from the fact that in the New Testament we have
the written counterpart of the apostolic paradosis, whilst the
apostolic paradosis itself is a preaching on the basis of the
Scriptures of the Old Testament. Three questions therefore
arise. First, what happens to the apostolic paradosis when it
takes the form of the paratheke? Second, what becomes of the
Scriptures when they are entrusted to the Church's safe-
keeping? Thirdly, Scripture as a form of the paratheke.

a) The apostolic paradosis in the form of the Church's tradition

Scripture is a form in which the apostolic paradosis, communicated to the Church, becomes the paratheke. The " sacred
writings " to which Paul refers Timothy (2 Tim 3 : 15) are in
fact, of course, the Old Testament writings, but we may also
apply them analogously to those of the New Testament. The
New Testament, that is, the works included in the Canon, are
a form in which the apostolic paradosis is entrusted to the
Church for safe-keeping. But the Canon of the New Testament
is not the only form in which the apostolic paradosis is
accessible to us. If we enunciate this thesis, we inevitably
involve ourselves in discussion with O. Cullmann regarding the
fact that the Church in the second century collected the various
individual " apostolic writings " into one whole, the Canon.

24

What was the significance of this? Cullmann regards it as follows: " By the introduction of the principle of a Canon, the Church recognized that from now on, tradition (that is to say, living tradition) was no criterion of truth. It drew a line under apostolic tradition and thereby declared that from now on, every later tradition must be tested by the apostolic tradition. In other words, that meant: ' Here is tradition which founds the Church and which imposes itself on the Church.' " Furthermore: " If the setting down in writing of the apostolic message is a fundamental fact of the incarnation, we have the right and duty to view apostolic tradition and the writings of the New Testament together, but on the other hand we must separate both from post-apostolic and post-canonical tradition." [34]

Nowadays there is agreement between the various denominations that New Testament Scripture is the written counterpart of apostolic tradition. We can also accept the view that apostolic is to be distinguished from post-apostolic tradition and that the latter must be tested by the former. But it can scarcely be supposed that the Church's intention in forming the Canon in the second century was to declare that here, and here alone, apostolic tradition was henceforth to be sought. By the principle of the Canon, the writings comprised in it were distinguished as genuinely " apostolic " writings from the apocryphal gospels and histories of apostles that had come into existence in the world of Gnosticism.[35] The Church did not do this arbitrarily, nor because these writings had imposed themselves on the Church solely by their inherent apostolic authority, but principally on the grounds that they had been used for a longer or shorter period in the public liturgical worship of the Church, in other words on the basis of tradition. For of course tradition is faithfully mirrored in the liturgy.[36] Augustine expresses this clearly : " If the (writings circulating) under the name of the apostles Andrew and John in fact came down from them, they would have been accepted in the Church which has persisted from their days down to our time through the quite certain succession of bishops." [37] If, however, the Canon of New Testament writings owes its existence expressly to the principle of tradition determining the Church, how could it be possible for the effect to put an end to the cause? The principle of the Canon did not mean the end of tradition in the Church, but its confirmation. If the formation of the Canon had the purpose which Cullmann attributes to it, this would necessarily have involved a decisive change in the teaching of the Fathers of that time regarding tradition. But no sign of that is perceptible. The theology of tradition continues uninterrupted from Irenaeus to Augustine despite the formation of the Canon. S. Dejaifve observes : " It cannot be proved, at least historically, that Scripture as the conclusion and fixing of the apostolic tradition put an end to living tradition. History gives quite a different picture. Precisely at the time when the New Testament took shape as the Canon of Holy Scripture, the magisterium charged the bishops to interpret Holy Scripture authentically, on the basis of the actual belief of the Churches and the *sensus ecclesiasticus,* the *phronema ekklesiastikon* ".[38]

Just as the living apostolic paradosis preceded its commitment to writing and ran parallel to this, so too did the collecting of the Scriptures into a Canon not put an end to it. It runs on uninterruptedly even after the formation of the Canon. But just as the apostolic ministry was perpetuated in the form of the apostolic, ecclesiastical office of the episcopate, so too was the apostolic paradosis perpetuated in the form of the Church's paradosis. In this way ecclesiastical paradosis joined sacred Scripture as the second form, independent of Scripture, of the paratheke entrusted to the Church. This independence of ecclesiastical paradosis is particularly brought out by Möhler. Behind it stands the Holy Spirit to whom the guidance and vivifying of the Church is entrusted and, according to the Tübingen theologian, it is the Spirit who forms the special Christian sense or tact in the human mind which receives the higher vital principle ever operative in the Church. In addition there is education by the successors of the apostles. The two together mean that " Scripture is not even absolutely necessary for its whole content to be received." [39] The Church's paradosis is the mode in which apostolic paradosis exists in the post-apostolic Church and exercises together with Scripture a necessary function in preserving the Gospel of Jesus Christ entrusted to the Church. For without the Church's paradosis the unity of faith and the uniform understanding of faith by the community of the faithful would be impossible and the Church as the one apostolic and Catholic teaching would be at an end.

b) The fate of apostolic paradosis in the Church's paradosis

What becomes of the Gospel of Jesus Christ transmitted by the apostolic paradosis when it assumes the mode of existence of ecclesiastical paradosis? We may say that in the latter the same thing happened to the Gospel of Jesus Christ and to the

Gospel regarding Jesus the Christ as had already happened in the apostolic paradosis. Just as what had once been spoken by Jesus, if it was to become a word spoken " here and now ", had to be subjected even in apostolic tradition to a change of form because of the changed situation, so too in ecclesiastical paradosis. The apostolic paradosis was concerned with proclaiming salvation in Jesus Christ and at the same time with the understanding of what was announced, in other words, with theology. That apostolic theology analysed from various points of view the inexhaustible riches of the mystery represented by Jesus Christ. So there was a Christology of the Suffering Servant, a *kenosis* Christology, one of glorification, one of death, and a resurrection Christology; there was a Galilean theology (of the name of Jesus), and a Jerusalem theology.[40] There was a different conception of the Gospel of Jesus Christ expressed by Paul and by the author of the fourth gospel; in other words, there was a distinctive Pauline and a distinctive Johannine theology. The specifically Galilean view of Christ as Jesus the descendant of David, together with the theology of glorification, led to a general conception of Jesus as the Christ, that is to say, to a definite community theology which Paul in Romans 1, 3 and 4 takes as the " Church paradosis ".[41] In 2 Timothy 2:8: " Remember Jesus Christ, risen from the dead, descended from David ", this theology already appears as what is probably a creed formula. Furthermore the importance of the opposition between Hebrews and Hellenists in the original Jerusalem Church was not restricted to the development and organic shaping of the Church but went deeper.[42] Behind it there was also a different conception of the preaching of Jesus the Christ, as Stephen's discourse shows

(Acts 6 : 8-60), for it is not in accordance with the usual mode of preaching the history of salvation. Here the different conceptions of sacred history and of the kerygma regarding Christ held by the Hebrews and the Hellenistic Jewish Christians of the Diaspora are evident.[43]

All this, which we have already noted in connection with the apostolic paradosis, continues in the Church's tradition. When the former was entrusted to the Church as a paratheke, for safe-keeping, that did not mean that the Church was to preserve the Gospel of life as a lifeless treasure. Franz von Baader was right in saying with regard to the Church's paradosis that though nothing might be altered, things could not stay as they were. The treasure of apostolic paradosis was not a mummy which after embalming was locked in a tomb and guarded. The striving for an ever deeper understanding of the Gospel within the Church, and the tendencies hostile to the Gospel which forced their way into the Church from outside, confronted those to whom the Gospel was entrusted with perpetually new situations and consequently with perpetually new tasks.

The apostolic tradition itself unfolded what Jesus Christ originally said. Thus the Suffering Servant Christology of the original Jerusalem community was not only completed by the Kyrios Christology of the Pauline kerygma, but finally displaced by it. The original form of post-apostolic tradition was the proclamation of Jesus as the Christ; it began with the man Jesus and brought out his significance for salvation by showing how after his death, Jesus was raised to be Lord and Christ (Acts 2 : 26). The subsequent development of this original doctrine, on the other hand, made it clear in detail what the precise significance of the man Jesus was. Now mention was made of Jesus' pre-earthly existence and his human life was expounded as the incarnation of the Son of God. Thus, for instance, in the piece of tradition used by Paul in Romans 1:1-4 the good news of his Son born of the seed of David according to the flesh predestinated the Son of God in power by reason of his resurrection from the dead. That is an actual exposition of the predicate, Son of God. For whilst Acts 13:33, 34 states that by raising Jesus from the dead, God fulfilled the promise: " You are my son, today I have begotten you " (Ps 2:7), and whilst this might possibly have been understood as though God had accepted, adopted, the man raised from the dead as his Son, the piece of tradition taken over by Paul in Romans 1:2-4 excludes such an adoptionist conception of the divine sonship by stating that the pre-existent Son of God was born of David's line according to the flesh. Furthermore the hymn of Philippians, another piece of tradition, places before the exaltation of the Messiah of the Petrine tradition the voluntary self-abasement into human existence of him who possessed God's mode of existence.

If the apostolic kerygma was to reach its hearers, the perpetually changing circumstances required it to be made in a form adapted to those circumstances. Only then was the word once spoken by the Lord truly the word which the Lord Jesus Christ was speaking in the particular situation actually confronting the Church; this is what we have already observed in the apostolic paradosis expressed in Scripture. When heretical conceptions of the Gospel arose in the Church, and when intellectual trends inimical to the Gospel invaded the Church, the Church faced again and again new contradictions which compelled it to clarify its doctrine in a form which took account of those contradictions and new questions. Thus one way of understanding the kerygma which had been possible before the contradictions arose was excluded. The formulation so arrived at represents the dialectical antithesis of the heresy. The doctrine preached now appears in a new garb of ideas and terms which represent an advance in understanding of the Gospel. And it is in no way a falsification of the Gospel and in particular of its character in relation to redemptive history, if the message of salvation is clothed in the garb of myth or if an attempt is made to obtain a better understanding of the mystery of Jesus Christ with the help of the concepts of Greek metaphysics.[44] In both cases, of course, the assistance of the human element of religious imagery and philosophical thought is called upon in order to throw light on what is divine, the mystery of the Incarnation. In this way the Gospel of Jesus Christ of necessity assumes in the Church's paradosis the form of *didaskalia,* of doctrine, just as, of course, Paul himself in his writings was conscious, in view of the false teachings arising in the Church, and in view of the false gnosis invading it (1 Tim 6:20), that he was no longer solely an apostle and herald of the message of Christ, but also a teacher of the gentiles (2 Tim 4:17). In the Church's paradosis, therefore, the apostolic paradosis is subjected to an historical process of continual interpretation.

c) Holy Scripture as a form of paratheke

What is the significance for the Church of the Scriptures that are entrusted to it as a paratheke? They are not something foreign to its nature, but are intended to contribute to shaping its life. They are necessary to the life of the Church; the only question is the precise extent of the necessity. Karl Rahner sees in Scripture an essential factor in the building of the Church: " By formal pre-definition of the kind that belongs to redemptive history and eschatology, God wills and provides Scripture as a constitutive factor in the foundation of the primitive Church." [45] In that case the " institution " of the Church by the historical Christ " cum apud nos degeret ", while he remained among us on earth, must be understood to mean that he laid the foundations of the Church, but that the resurrection and the sending of the Spirit themselves also essentially belong to the building of the Church. Then there is no intrinsic impossibility in including the operation of the Holy Spirit inspiring the sacred writers, that is to say, the coming into existence of the Scriptures, as a constitutive factor among the acts that went to build the Church. [46]

But what is constitutive of the Church is the proclamation of the Gospel by the apostles, the *viva vox evangelii per apostolos*. Scripture, on the other hand, serves within the Church (together with the Church's tradition) " ut sublatis erroribus puritas ipsa evangelii in ecclesia conservetur " (Conc. Trid. Session IV, Denzinger 783). In other words, Scripture has no constitutive significance for the authentic and doctrinally authoritative testimony to the Gospel; it is rather " post iactum fidei confessionis fundamentum ", a " potissimum testimonium ac praesidium in confirmandis dogmatibus " (ibid., Denzinger 784). And this formula *in confirmandis dogmatibus* is all the more weighty because the Council changed the phrase *in constituendis dogmatibus,* which is what already stood in the draft, into *in confirmandis dogmatibus*. In short, the Council of Trent clearly circumscribed the function of Scripture: it has to serve the Church for the maintenance and confirmation of its kerygma. Though we said above that there was never any preaching without holy Scripture, and cited the example of the original apostolic kerygma, the use of Old Testament prophecy by the apostles had no constitutive significance for their kerygma regarding Jesus the Christ, but only a confirmative one; it only served to support and confirm what the apostles were preaching about Jesus, namely, that in him as the Messiah, Old Testament prophecy had found its fulfilment. Scripture was given to the Church by the Holy Spirit as one of the two forms of the paratheke, so that the Church might preserve the purity of the Gospel and confirm its kerygma, but not for it to derive the object of its preaching from Scripture in the first place.

How does the Church do justice to this task of faithfully preserving the sacred Scriptures committed to its care? In the first place it collects them into a whole and gives this whole collection a regulative significance. In this way the collection became the Canon of Scripture. There is no doubt that the act of making this collection involved a process of selection.[47] What criterion did the Church employ? That of explicit revelation cannot be proved, at most may be postulated. Certainly the criterion of " authenticity " was operative, seeing that the gospels included in the Canon and the Acts of the Apostles were distinguished from the apocryphal gnostic gospels and the Acta Thomae, Andreae, Pauli, etc. But that was probably not the sole criterion. For the question must be raised whether the Church did not also extend its process of selection to the genuine " apostolic " and therefore inspired writings, too. If that were the case, some inspired writings were not taken by the Church into its Canon. Is it conceivable that the process of selection carried out by the Church in forming the Canon of the New Testament also extended to inspired writings?

We can only answer this difficult question after making certain observations such as the following. The Gospel according to Matthew, originally composed in Aramaic, was replaced by its Greek version, and has not been preserved. It is impossible, however, to prove that the original Aramaic Matthew was not inspired. We learn from the introduction to Luke's gospel (Lk. 1-4) that when he set about its composition, he had a fair number of gospels available. He evidently not only read these, but used them, and it would be a mistake to try to read into this preface of his own gospel a criticism of those earlier gospels, as Eusebius did (*Church History* 3, 24), and as has often been done since. On the contrary, according to Luke, those gospels were good, only his own was to be better, in the first place because he had carefully investigated all that had happened " from the beginning ", and consequently was in a position to offer something new, and also because his gospel was written in a style capable of satisfying more exacting demands.[48] Whether these gospels were written by eye-witnesses or whether they were based on the reports of eye-witnesses, as Luke's gospel was, cannot be determined from what Luke says, nor whether they were written by collaborators of the apostles or not, nor whether they were in use in the various local communities of the original apostolic Church or not. But what prevents us from assuming that they too were " apostolic " writings just as Luke's gospel was, that they were the memoirs of men who had followed the apostles (cf. Justin, I *Apol.* 67)? Furthermore, between our First and Second canonical Letters to the Corinthians, Paul sent by Titus the so-called " severe letter " to the Church of Corinth (2 Cor 2:4), and this does not appear in the Canon of the New Testament.[49] Was it lost? Was it considered inappropriate for reception into the Church's Canon? Was it partly incorporated into the Second Letter to the Corinthians? Nobody is in a position to decide. Luke's gospel belongs to inspired Scripture. The " severe letter ", being the letter of an apostle, must be considered inspired. And who can prove that the pre-Lucan gospels, the " apostolic " character of which cannot necessarily be gainsaid, were not inspired? On the contrary, we can indicate a reason drawn from the nature of inspiration itself which would make it acceptable to consider that they were in fact inspired.

The *Spiritus inspirator* is none other than the *Spiritus creator*. But the creator Spirit in the profusion of his generosity brings forth millions upon millions of blossoms of which only a relatively small number come to fruition. Could not something similar hold good of the *Spiritus inspirator* as regards inspired writings, especially in view of the charismata in the first age of the Church? There was no reason for him to be niggardly or calculating. Furthermore, inspiration leaves the human author who is the instrument of the Holy Spirit the full freedom of his personality and individuality, and consequently his historical limitations. And it is this aspect of inspiration that makes it an historical process, so that if this idea is applied to the genesis of our present gospels, it may be

35

said that the canonical gospels represent the mature final stage and fruit of a previous development, represented by antecedent forms of the gospels. The flowers, however, or gospels which were available to Luke, would be of the same kind as the fruit; in other words, we have reason to assume that they can be regarded as inspired. The best, however, is the enemy of the good. Consequently, only our present canonical gospels found a place in liturgical worship and then, because they were inspired writings in public use, found their way into the Church's Canon. The Canon of Scripture was therefore formed by the Church, and what was decisive was the Church's paradosis, above all the liturgical use of these writings; it was not fixed on the basis of a special revelation of God to the apostles regarding the extent of the Canon. The Canon has not its source in a divine act of revelation but is purely a product of the Church which to be sure was endowed with infallibility in the matter. From the fact, however, that the formation of the Canon was an act of the Church itself, two inferences may be drawn. In the first place its formation involved a process of selection, and the Canon therefore does not claim to include all inspired writings. It only says that the inspired writings contained in it have a regulative significance in the Church and for the Church.[50] Secondly, if the extent of the Canon had been made known by God through revelation, this must have happened before the death of the last apostle. In that case no writing of a collaborator of the apostles or of the disciples of an apostle which was written after the death of the last apostle could have been considered inspired and therefore capable of inclusion in the Canon, unless it had been revealed to the apostles which writings that were to be com-

36

posed after their death by their disciples were to belong to the Canon. " Yet not only can no trace of such a revelation be shown to exist, but there is much reason to suppose that it did not. Nor is it presupposed by any official doctrinal pronouncement of the Church, and it is as good as excluded by the course taken by the history of the Canon." [51] But if the extent of the Canon is not derived from revelation but was in fact established solely by the Church, by a purely ecclesiastical act, then there is nothing to prevent a work composed after the death of the apostles, but still belonging to the apostolic period, from being received into the Canon of Scripture. All that this decides in principle regarding the question of the authors of the canonical writings is that they must have belonged to the apostolic period of the Church.

Holy Scripture as the guardian of the Gospel is the dowry of the Holy Spirit to the Bride of Christ, the most precious jewel in which the *Spiritus creator* endowed her subsequent life with the word of Christ. The faith, prayer and preaching of the Church are henceforward nourished and animated, as though by God's breath, by the Gospel which is announced by Christ the Church's Lord, preached by the apostles its foundation, and borne witness to by the Holy Spirit who caused it to be written down by the sacred writers. The Scriptures were given to the Church so that it could preserve the Gospel entrusted to it. " But continue then in those things which thou hast learned and which have been committed to thee. Knowing of whom thou hast learned them " (2 Tim 3:14). They are also to lead the Church to its goal: " From childhood you have been acquainted with the sacred writings which are able to instruct you for salvation through faith in Jesus Christ "

37

(2 Tim 3:15). They are to serve the Church to enable it to fulfil its manifold tasks, for " all scripture is inspired by God and profitable for teaching, for reproof, for correction and for training in righteousness " (2 Tim 3: 16). Holy Scripture is, therefore, the Church's " heart's blood, its very breath, its soul, its all ".[52]

II

THE PROBLEM OF PRIMITIVE REVELATION AND TRADITION IN NINETEENTH CENTURY THEOLOGY

1. *Introduction*

With the question of tradition we encounter the foundations of our faith and Church life, for the Church is based on the principle of living tradition. It is not surprising that tradition has become one of the most topical problems of the present day, and not only within the limits of the Catholic Church. " It is highly significant that in recent years the problem of tradition has become a frequent theme for works of theological research both among Protestants and Roman Catholics." [1] The theology of the Lutheran and Reformed Churches too has turned away from the extreme " Scripture alone " principle of seventeenth century Protestant orthodoxy. Tradition has become a serious problem for that theology, not only because the denominational climate has changed, so that people no longer attack one another but listen to one another, take one another seriously and engage in mutual discussion, but ultimately for an objective reason, the recognition of the historical character of our life as human beings and as believers. And so our intellectual situation has altered completely; after all, even recently, when the Church referred the faithful to living tradition, it found itself in contradiction to an outlook which could only see in tradition something obsolete, superseded, a constraint and restriction on the freedom of the individual. To tradition men opposed liberty and the optimistic belief in progress, not only in the age of the Enlightenment, but right down into the early twentieth century, until the rapture of freedom and the optimistic belief in progress came to an abrupt end with the catastrophe of the first world war. This was followed by an even worse catastrophe which ended with the complete collapse of Germany in the second world war and unleashed a nihilism of despair.

This is the situation which explains the search for support and security in a firm tradition and which was to bring about a substantial advance in the struggle for tradition. For now it was no longer simply tradition in the sphere of Christianity and the Church which was in question, but natural tradition, too, which forms the basis of supernatural tradition. For of course there is tradition not only in the realm of revelation and faith, but in the natural field of human existence generally. In fact without this natural tradition rooted in the nature of man, supernatural tradition based on revelation would lack any firm point of contact in men and would, as it were, remain in the air. If the Church's principle of tradition is nevertheless widely rejected, the reason is that our intellectual development since Descartes has destroyed the intellectual foundations of tradition. It would take too long to show in detail how this came about. We may perhaps refer the reader to the detailed analyses of Gerhardt Krüger.[2] In view of the material and intellectual ruins which we owe to autonomous man—and behind them also stand the " leaders ", with their absolute authority in the totalitarian states—our intellectual situation inevitably appears as " that of an epoch struck by the calamitous fate of the loss of tradition generally, the disappearance of support and security, the collapse of stability, an asphyxiating void and the destruction of the very element of mental life." [3] With disturbing prophetic gaze people discern the grim nihilism which lurks behind a life that rejects all natural tradition. " If tradition were really wholly eliminated, nihilism would be complete; if there were nothing at all that still stood firm, there would be no longer any possibility whatever of appealing to fundamentals of our common humanity, taken for granted as a matter of course." [4]

If, then, tradition is what remains identical in the course of historical change, it is clear that historical change belongs to its essence and is the animating, progressive factor in it. If the latter is lacking, what persists becomes something rigid, lifeless and mechanical, a conservatism that does not understand the signs of the times and which can be just as fatal as the loss of all stability and the asphyxiation of a void. On the other hand, too great a strain seems to be laid on the concept of tradition if its decisive significance is thought to consist in " the handing on from the beginning exclusively of what is received, that is, of what by its very origin is something received ".[5] That is not valid of tradition as such, but only of a certain kind of tradition, for example, the Mosaic Jewish and Christian traditions, and the tradition of primitive revelation, if such a thing is assumed to have been there. Manners, customs and habits form in human social structures (families, tribes, peoples), which, once they exist, persist and so become traditions; local costumes, for example, which die out or are only worn on festive occasions and laid aside afterwards. In such cases, nothing that goes right back to the beginning is handed down, and yet they exemplify tradition in the true sense of the word. It may also be doubted whether there is no place for progress here. Local costumes can be adapted to the age, but if they are preserved in essentials, they remain what they are, that is, clothes determined by tradition and custom. Tradition is something living and consequently capable of, and calling for, adaptation. The situation is, of course, different when it is a question of truth: to alēthes[6]. But this is a special case of tradition. And a further essential element of tradition is freedom, as Gerhardt Ebeling in particular has pointed out.[7] Certainly free choice and decision here is not unrestricted, for it can only be made within the area prescribed by tradition. Ebeling rightly notes that " tradition is predetermined decision." [8] We shall see later that there are various attitudes in relation to tradition, in which there can be no question of free, inner affirmation, the conformist attitude for instance. The individual human being, within the domain of a tradition, may positively accept it out of genuine conviction; he may accept it passively as something more or less burdensome and behave in external conformity to it without inward assent; he can also reject it, accepting the consequence of being regarded as an outsider: it is always tradition which makes anyone seem an outsider. Then it can be a matter of usage, or of certain forms of community, of religion, of structures which are characterized by the fact that, as the past crystallized, they limit the scope of present living, and so on account of their provenance in some respect shape the future in advance. History is an essential factor in tradition. It ensures that preservation does not become rigidity, a lifeless mindless conservatism. On the other hand, the continuity that characterizes tradition preserves the historical element from disintegrating into purely subjective individual views of the world, of religion and of knowledge, and so from destroying the common cultural, religious and mental domain, with the result that humanity would simply cease to be human. Now that we have reached the end of " modern times ", reflection is being directed to the preceding period of the Western mind. People now recognize in it " a particularly changeable epoch, with a preference for change, a particularly restless and revolutionary age ", the determining law of which was historical mutability. People realize the danger that what is newly created has no lasting value; that with what is perpetually new, continuity in the course of history is lost, together with the identity of what endures through change, substantial identity, that is, so that only one absolute is left, mutability. Yet mere mutability distorts the nature of history. There is no absolute mutability; change always presupposes the identity of something which changes in the course of history and nevertheless remains itself in the course of historical transformations. But that is exactly what we mean by tradition. " Thus history as unity and connection presupposes a tradition." If tradition is broken, a new history begins. " History and tradition belong together." [9] Pieper completes this by not taking as his starting point the content of what is handed down, but by trying to determine the nature of tradition on the basis of the act of transmission. In the act of tradition, however, something that one has oneself received is communicated, something is handed on, as the English expression shows in its two forms, " to hand down from ", and " to hand down to ". Something is passed on which had previously been received,[10] the one action being the necessary correlative of the other. Only so is the act of tradition complete.

That is correct, but needs qualification. It is not universally true that the decisive element in the concept of tradition consists in " the handing on from the beginning exclusively of what is received, that is, of what by its very origin is something received ";[11] this only holds in certain cases. Habits and customs form in human social structures (families, tribes, peoples), which endure by being taken over by later generations, but they can also die out. This is true even of customs within the Church. Thus, for example, the wearing of veils by women at divine service (St. Paul) still exists to some extent in southern countries but has disappeared in the north. In all such cases nothing that " by its very origin is something received " is transmitted. This latter is a special case, and whether even in this case there is no place for progress can also be doubted. The concept of tradition must not be rigid. It is something living and therefore capable of adaptation. It is a different matter when truth (*to alēthes*)[12] is in question. But here too, linked to the persistence of what is received, there is the historical factor and therefore the mutability of its perpetually new, profounder understanding or even of perpetual defection from it.

With truth, a further element in tradition appears, authority.

For tradition and authority are linked here. Without authority there is no tradition concerning what is true. But who are the bearers of this authority and what is it based on? It is founded on the transmitter's standing nearer to the source of what is received. This is indicated by the names given to the vehicles of tradition: *antiqui*, *maiores*, forbears, *hoi palaioi*, *hoi archaioi*,[13] " those close to the wellspring, the early ones, those at the beginning ",[14] those acquainted with the truth, *to alēthes autoi isasin*,[15] who relieve us of the anxiety of being concerned with the opinions of men, whose wisdom is on everyone's lips.[16] The authority of the ancients is founded on the fact that they have received knowledge from a divine source and hand on what they have so received.[17]

Tradition is therefore always alive and is never of merely historical interest, and the reason is that knowledge of what is close to the origin is a gift of the gods (*theon dōsis*), not something acquired for oneself. Those who " are better than we and nearer to the gods, have handed down this knowledge to us ",[18] a thought that recurs in Cicero, for whom too the time of origins is nearest to the gods. He was concerned " ritus familiae patrumque servare ", is " quoniam antiquitas proxime accedit ad Deos, a Diis quasi traditam religionem tueri ".[19] For Cicero, religion was given by the gods and we are to keep and protect it. The *archaioi* were inspired by the gods; hence their authority. But we should not refer to the inspired authors of holy Scripture as an analogous case;[20] for with them inspiration concerns only the writing down of what has already been revealed. Pieper is right in distinguishing the obligatory character of " tradition " from other obligations towards what has been handed down such as the cultural heritage of a

45

nation. Although Alexander Rüstow, for example, maintains that on authority, respect, trust and reverence the social continuity of civilization from generation to generation depends, so that those who undermine these feelings subvert the ultimate foundation of human civilization,[21] nevertheless there cannot be any absolute obligation in regard to this kind of tradition, if for no other reason than that every new generation adds something new of its own. Only the central cell of a people's civilization, the sacred tradition, must be taken over and handed on without alteration, because it springs from a divine source and is needed by every generation; nor can any individual, whatever his genius, add anything comparable to it. Only when this tradition is no longer handed on is there a breach with and loss of tradition. And even the loss of religious customs in the family—Pieper mentions that of making the sign of the Cross over a loaf before cutting it—is not a loss of tradition as long as men hold fast to the sacred tradition which absolutely has to be maintained. This latter is, therefore, not to be confused with the cultivation of so-called "traditions", for the latter often amounts to a superannuated conservatism, which can even be an obstacle to the preservation of genuine tradition. Yet such customs also have their profound significance, for they are the historical husks which have formed protectively round the kernel of tradition, preserving it and linking it to concrete circumstance, so that anyone who throws away these husks runs the risk of forfeiting the kernel as well.

As historical forms of sacred tradition, Pieper lists: Christian doctrinal tradition, mythical tradition, which he regards as an echo of primitive revelation, and finally, primitive revelation.

As regards the latter, Pieper complains that the average arbitrarily narrow theological concept of tradition, in contradiction to its own presuppositions, does not expressly include the sacred tradition based on original revelation, the remains of which are met with, he thinks, in the myths of the various nations.[22] We shall have to speak of the handing down of myths later. Pieper is not criticizing theology as such, but scholastic theology in which the fundamental idea implied by primitive revelation plays no very great role. But as well as scholastic theology, there are other forms of theology, and they have concerned themselves in detail with primitive revelation and, as a consequence, with tradition. A philosopher like Pieper cannot be expected to be acquainted with them in detail; a theologian may therefore be permitted to indicate them. Thus the theologian Franz Geiger of Lucerne (1755-1843) was a representative of Traditionalism. His theology was a synthesis of French Traditionalism and German philosophical Romanticism. It was in fact the latter which regarded the various particular expressions of religion as symbols of an original revelation.[23] This was reinforced by French Traditionalism in opposition to the Enlightenment and the Revolution. For Geiger, the individual intellect in the concrete is not, as the Enlightenment would have it, a creative, self-sufficient organ, but essentially a receptive, assimilating organ, the eye of the mind, sensitive to light. " Our reason is the eye of the mind. Just as our bodily eye sees nothing if it does not receive light from nature, so too our intellectual eye (our reason) sees nothing if it does not receive light from the highest (absolute) reason. Our reason is the power to grasp truth." [24] Consequently communication from the absolute reason by the organ of revelation is the only possible way in which humanity attains reason, directly in the organ of revelation and its manifestation, indirectly through tradition: " We have revelation alone to thank for our rationality." [25] " If nothing is imparted to man, he never becomes rational." [26] Cain and his race are a warning example that to abandon tradition involves sinking into unreason and savagery. " Cain too had his reason, but it did not in fact shine for him of itself; for when after murdering his brother he fled from his father, he no longer heard the supreme reason which had revealed itself to his father to be conveyed in turn to his sons; as a result he became wild and irrational, and his race became more and more unreasonable." [27]

The form in which the revelation of the absolute reason is presented cannot, however, be that of writing, for the use of writing obviously presupposes a certain level of civilization and cannot be a generally available means of understanding, and also because all writing, merely in itself by its very nature, is ambiguous. Revelation is only conveyed unambiguously by word of mouth. But what is the basis of the transmission of revelation by this means unambiguously and without falsification? In himself the man handing on tradition is merely an individual mind among others of the most varied grades and levels of culture or lack of it. Must this not inevitably result in the revelation's becoming indefinite and bearing many meanings? The reason why this does not occur is that the bearer of the tradition is accredited by God. " The oral spokesmen must be persons authenticated by God himself, for only such people can guarantee us the truth." [28] Tradition and authority go together.

2. *Johann Sebastian von Drey* (1777-1853)

It was above all the Catholic Tübingen school, however, which acknowledged an original revelation and, as a corollary, Traditionalism. Its founder, Johann Sebastian von Drey, showed himself an adherent of Traditionalism from the very beginning of his academic teaching in Ellwangen as is clear from his manuscript work: *Ideen zur Geschichte des katholischen Dogmensystems. Mit Benützung von Münschers Handbuch dargestellt* 1812/13.[29] Here he expresses the conviction "that for the highest, that is to say religious, development and formation, a direct divine instruction, a direct divine revelation was necessary."[30] Revelation is not a special, separate area inside the world of religion, only realized in the redemptive history of Israel and Christianity. It comprises all religions. And so Drey forms the idea of " an all-embracing revelation ",[31] and this in clear connection with Lessing (as his diary confirms); he accepts the idea of an eternal divine educative plan extending through the whole history of humanity and manifested in the history of religion in general and, in a perfect form, in Christianity. According to Drey, therefore, revelation from its original form onwards undergoes a development which reaches its culmination in Christianity. The world of religion is supported by a revelation which pursues its course " in secret ", by God's ceaseless operation.[32] In the justification of religion which he works out, accomplishing the change-over from experience as Schleiermacher had conceived it, to Traditionalism,[33] Drey comes to the conclusion that " all original religion is revealed ".[34]

This principle, which Drey developed in his *Ideen zum*

katholischen Dogmensystem (1812/13) and in his essay of
1826, is given a detailed proof in his *Apologetik als wissen-
schaftliche Nachweisung der Göttlichkeit des Christentums
in seiner Erscheinung* (Mainz 1843, ²1847). "The original
religion by original revelation ",[35] according to him, manifests
itself in the ancient stories and traditions of the nations as a
basic fact, and consequently testifies to a more or less instinctive
grasp, even in that early stage of the world, of what we know
by clear thought to be necessary. Drey appeals particularly
to the testimony of holy Scripture in the " first and oldest
traditions " in which is described how the first human beings
developed their awareness of God, as well as the first elements
of their religious feeling, by God's assistance and under his
direct guidance, so that religion was originally mediated, and
became a reality, by revelation. The form of thought and
representation in holy Scripture proves to him the great
antiquity and originality of this tradition. " God appears to
man visibly in the midst of nature like a natural being;
cultivates man's society like a father with his children, forms
and educates him in an equally paternal way, teaches him
what he may do and what he must not, draws his attention
to the consequences of his action in order to warn him against
harm and misfortune and finally reveals to the man who did
not heed his warning the further consequences of his trans-
gression, without however depriving him of his consolation
and help ".[36] This is how the original revelation is described.
The fall, however, brought about the division of men, in
particular that of the impious (the descendants of Cain) from
the pious (those of Seth), and this is repeated at each new
stage.[37] Among the descendants of Seth, the original revelation

50

assumed the form of family religion, which further developed the original revelation, which had consisted in society with God himself, and became a mediate one, in the form of faith. In the family, however, more than in any other social structure, the guarding and preserving element in tradition is characteristic. Among the Sethites, therefore, the original revelation continued to live by tradition from generation to generation in the form of family religion, with the original religion advancing and developing from immediacy to a form mediated by faith, and striving to maintain and propagate this,[38] whilst the impious sank into brutality.[39]

If family tradition was the bulwark that protected the primitive revelation, tradition entered a new stage with the coalescence of the tribes into a nation after the Deluge. Drey explains this stage on the basis of the Romantic concept of the characteristic national spirit of each people. Accordingly the rise of the different nations necessarily brings about change and differentiation in religion, and therefore in tradition, just as the universally human element in a nation takes concrete form in the special characteristics of the various peoples. Just as it is impossible for a nation to be distinct from others without the language which corresponds to its own characteristics, so too is this impossible without the differentiation and development of its own religion. The division of the nations necessarily leads to manifold developments in them, and consequently to a division of religion.[40] The help of original revelation was necessary for the development at the very beginning; by it, to some extent at least, humanity attained religious concepts. That circle of religious ideas became the basis of all further development. When the great migrations of the

Germanic nations began, the common good which all preserved as a legacy was their original religion and it was the
starting point of all further developments. With the emergence
into consciousness of what characterized each people, it was
inevitable that corresponding notions were formed of the
primitive revelation. Out of what was originally the single
religion of all, there came the various national religions corresponding to the spirit of each people.

In this, " tradition and its content was the starting point for
all further developments among the nations ".[41] This explains
how the content of this common tradition, religious and
historical memories (e.g. the Flood), recur in the ancient stories
of nearly all peoples, in many different forms, it is true, and
always shaped to suit each particular nation, yet with least loss
in this transformation.[42]

3. Johann Adam Möhler (1796-1838)

A year earlier than Drey, his pupil Johann Adam Möhler
had already adopted Traditionalism in his early work *Die
Einheit in der Kirche oder das Prinzip des Katholizismus,
dargestellt im Geiste des Kirchenväter der drei ersten Jahrhun-
derte* (1825, ²1843).[43] For him it was " quite definite from the
start that there is no knowledge of God without special revelation ".[44] By this the young theologian professes Traditionalism.
It is true that the young Möhler gives this Traditionalism a
Romantic stamp by making union with the universe a condition of man's knowledge of God, and at the same time it has
a note of conscious hostility to the Enlightenment. " He who

created the whole can only be known from the whole, because only in the whole does he reveal himself." [45] The way Möhler solves the question of man's knowledge of God shows a radical overcoming of the Enlightenment conception of man. If independent individual thought was the first demand of the Enlightenment, for the Romantic Möhler that was almost equivalent to atheism. So little was he satisfied with the independent, self-sufficient individual and his independent thought, that in regard to the knowledge of God the latter must necessarily end in atheism : " Man if completely separated (from all society) would not have any God at all, for he would be similar to himself." [46]

The ways in which Möhler solves the question of man's knowledge of God are the precise contraries of those in which the Enlightenment had reached its solution of the problem of God. They correspond to his view of man. And his view is that of Romantic entheism. The foundation of his teaching regarding man's knowledge of God is his metaphysics of man's immanence in God. By this Möhler understood man's union with the universe, which mediates his immanence in God. But this union with the universe is not only man's true being in God, but it is " the condition of true knowledge of God, the creator of the universe ".[47] And this applies to the universe in its objective as well as in its subjective aspect. The universe is on the one hand the objective condition which makes it possible for man to know God, for the universe has its ground in God. When reference is made to immanence in God, therefore, it is the immanence of the universe in God which is meant. Man possesses his immanence in God only through the universe, as a member of the universe. The reason why the universe is the objective condition of man's knowledge of God is that, having its ground in God, the universe is at the same time the whole revelation of God. The universe is the totality of God's revelations, the ways in which God manifests himself universally and reveals himself wholly. That means, therefore, that the universe in its objective aspect is " the condition of the true knowledge of God, the creator of the universe ". But on the other hand this also holds good of the subjective aspect. God is not known by the individual only from the total universe as God's total revelations, " but he can only be known by the individual in the whole ".[48] " Only from the whole can he who created the whole be known, because he only reveals himself in the whole." That means, then, that the universe is not only the object by which God is known, but also the subject through which God is known. This indicates the way by which the individual human being arrives at the knowledge of God, namely, by becoming the whole in a certain fashion; though he is not the whole, he " expands to the whole ".

How can this be, however? The way in which Möhler solves this problem shows him to be the complete Romantic. It takes place by love, which breaks down the limits of the individual and equates him with the whole. " In love, we individual beings become co-extensive with the whole." So the individual, through love, knows what the whole knows; it is therefore love which grasps God. " How is the individual to know him? By the fact that although he cannot *be* the whole, he can nevertheless comprise it in his love, great-heartedly; and although he *is* not the whole, the whole is nevertheless in him, and he knows what the whole (knows)." Consequently the knowledge of God is only possible to man inasmuch as he is a member of the universe and as long as he remains a member of the universe.

As, however, the universe is represented for us men by humanity, the individual can only know God to the extent that he is and remains a member of mankind as a whole. Just as Möhler develops the knowledge of God as the creator of the universe from the metaphysics of man's immanence in God, so too does he develop the non-recognition of God by man from the metaphysics of man's separation of himself from the universe. Accordingly, all non-recognition of God is based on man's cutting himself off from the whole and so failing in his vocation to be a member of the universe. So little does this Romantic among the theologians consider the autonomous individual of the Enlightenment view of man truly to represent the nature of man that it is precisely by being separate and individual that the fall from God is accomplished. For what is the autonomous, self-sufficient individual, if not man detaching himself from the whole, cutting himself off from the whole and making himself the centre? But that is precisely what constitutes the nature of sin. For such separation is equivalent to falling from God. For if union with the universe is at the same time existence in God, the latter is lost if man abandons his unity with the universe; the very condition of knowing God as the creator of the universe is destroyed. Man can only know God from the totality of the universe as the totality of his revelations, and this by opening out his heart in love to the whole universe. When man separates himself from the whole, that is equivalent to his placing himself above the whole, depreciating the whole and abasing the whole; his heart does not go out to the whole but shrinks into itself. Consequently he abases the whole to himself, with the result that he himself wishes to be all in all and refers everything egotistically to himself as centre. Instead of man expanding to comprise all things through love, and then contemplating all things in himself, he now projects himself into all things. And so we know only what a part knows, and contemplate of God only as much as the proportionate part of the whole which we are. " Therefore there can no longer be one God and creator of all men." For " the one creator is only recognized as one in unity with his whole creation ". Consequently as many gods must be made as there are men. It is not the case, therefore, that the fall from God is the consequence of our knowledge of God becoming faulty. On the contrary, the dimming of our awareness of God is the consequence of a prior fall from God, which must already have taken place. It occurs by our separating ourselves from the universe, for God is only given in and through the universe as the totality of his revelations. To separate ourselves from the universe is to separate ourselves from immanence in God. And when by pride we place ourselves over the whole, we also place ourselves above God. When we abase the whole, God too is " dragged down, depreciated, until, as history shows, he is placed on the same level with man or man with him ". The fall from God has taken place, and in the end there is either the humanization of God or the divinization of man. Conversely, true knowledge of God has as its condition man's membership of the universe and man's consequent immanence in God. The individual human being can truly know God " only in the universe, by living in it and embracing it whole-heartedly ".

The world, the universe, confronts man directly in the form

of mankind, for to man this represents the universe. " For us the universe is represented by humanity." Consequently life in the whole universe amounts for man, primarily and directly, to life in the human community; to separate oneself from the whole or to place oneself above the whole is equivalent to detaching oneself from the community of men and placing oneself above it. Complete separation from the human community, the completely autonomous individual, is therefore equivalent to complete godlessness. " A fully separate man would have no God at all, for he would be similar to himself." [49] There is so necessary a connection for this Romantic between universe and humanity on one side and the *one* God and creator of the universe on the other, between some form of human society and the divine, that complete and consistent egotism, that is to say, rigorously logical individualism, is equivalent to atheism, whereas whenever there is some community, there is also something divine. Wherever particular groups take shape and form, they have a common world of gods. The disintegration of the single community of mankind involves, it is true, the loss of the grandiose union with the entire creation and consequently of the knowledge of the *one* God. To the extent at least that this one community has split into a number of communities, the nations, the one God has been divided into a multiplicity of gods, and " circumscribed ". Yet to the extent that the nations are forms of society, they have at least retained something divine. " When the individual at least contemplates himself in a nation, the possibility exists of his having a limited and human god, but at any rate a god." [50] It is clear, therefore, that the single isolated individual cannot know God; he is egotism personified. A man's total self-isolation is equivalent to complete atheism. The knowledge of God occurs only in a community. To the degree that man breaks out of his egotism, widens his heart to comprise the community in his love, the possibility also increases for him to know God. The *one* God and creator of the universe, however, can only be known in community with the whole of mankind. Man only knows the one God when he is a member of all mankind.

What does this actually mean? What does Möhler mean by saying that what is impossible to the individual is possible to the whole of mankind and that the individual through knowing in conjunction with the whole of mankind can attain what must remain inaccessible to him as an individual? Is Möhler ascribing at any rate to the whole of humanity what he is refusing to the individual? Does he mean that the whole of mankind with its inherent cognitive powers is able of itself to know the one God and creator of the universe? By no means. His declared opposition to the naturalism of the Enlightenment makes it impossible for him to maintain this, which of course would amount to a knowledge of God by an autonomous self-sufficient mankind and consequently to the destruction of the " perpetual and living connection of mankind with God ". When Möhler attributes to mankind as a whole the knowledge of the one God and creator of all things, it must never be taken to mean that the knowledge of God is the act of mankind alone, for that would contradict his metaphysics of the divine ground of mankind's being. It would also contradict Möhler's concept of reason, which for him is a receptive organ. For Möhler, as for Jacobi, Sailer and the French Traditionalists, human reason is the power of perception. It is the side of the human mind which is open towards God and ready to receive. There belongs to mankind as such a need of the divine, a longing and feeling for the divine. In it is the basis and inner capacity, not indeed to advance towards the knowledge of God by its own strength, but to receive the true knowledge of God.[51] For mankind to come to know about God, the revealing act of God himself is necessary. All knowledge about God is knowledge through God and is derived from God himself by his revealing himself in the universe and through the universe. But we know that for man the universe is represented by mankind. Therefore the individual can only come to the knowledge of God by God's revealing himself in and through mankind.

What form does this revelation of God take? It is a " special " revelation. For Möhler, it is established " from the start " that without special revelation there is no knowledge of God.[52] This special revelation consists in God's having spoken his word and with his word, his name, into mankind. Wherever the name of God is named among mankind, it was first given to mankind by God's own revelation, whether it was in the original revelation at the beginning of human history, or whether particular truths were communicated to chosen men by the Logos operative even in the pagan world, or whether, finally, it occurred through revelation in Jesus Christ.[53] Mankind therefore does not know God by its own cognitive powers, but is rather only an organ receptive to God's special revelation in the Word. It is also the organ which retains the knowledge about God conveyed to it by the word of God. As, however, the word of God has been addressed to the whole of mankind by the one God and creator of all things,

59

that whole of mankind alone can maintain and preserve this word in its purity. Now we understand why Möhler writes: " Only from the whole can he who created the whole be known ".[54] It means that only if the individual human being opens himself out to mankind as a whole, by love, is he capable of receiving within him and of affirming for his own part the word of God about the one God and creator of the universe which has been spoken to the whole of mankind. Opposition to the Deist solution of the problem of God thus led Möhler, in agreement with his master Drey, to the traditionalist view of man's knowledge of God. Man " receives " faith in the divine which is " handed down ", and then hands it on himself. Möhler remained faithful in principle to this solution through all the stages of his theological development.

This Romantically-coloured Traditionalism was clarified and deepened by Möhler ten years later. He had another opportunity of expressing his views on the question in a letter to Bautain in March 1835.[55] The new problem was the relation of Traditionalism to the various forms of proof of the existence of God. The way in which Möhler deals with the question entitles us to regard him from that date onwards as holding a moderate Traditionalism. The occasion of the letter was the conflict in which the Strasbourg philosopher Bautain had become involved with the Bishop of Strasbourg, J. Fr. Lepappe de Trévern, on account of his extreme Traditionalism.[56] The trend of his thought can be seen from his starting point, natural knowledge in the immediate form of natural faith.

What does Möhler understand by the natural knowledge of God by fallen man? There can be no doubt what was meant when the Bishop of Strasbourg affirmed that reasoning alone (*le raisonnement seul*) is sufficient to make it possible to prove with certainty the existence of the creator and his infinite perfection.[57] As opposed to Möhler's view,[58] it signified in the scholastic sense a mediate inference by human reason of the existence of the supreme being from the facts of the world seen as his effects, such as Aquinas presents in classical form in the Five Ways of the Summa.[59] For Möhler's interpretation of human existence before God on the basis of reason, it is very instructive, however, to see what attitude he adopts to the objections of the Bishop of Strasbourg. He considers that the question is simply what the whole natural man without grace —in short, what nature *alone*—is capable of. The bishop's expression *par le raisonnement seul* must not, he says, be taken in the strict and narrow sense, for the bishop had no intention of distinguishing between understanding and reason, mediate and immediate knowledge. There was no question of precisely what natural power of the mind attains the " natural knowledge " of God, or whether that knowledge is ultimately mediate or immediate. The mode of this rational knowledge could even be a direct rational knowledge, a rational faith. In that case, that would be the required rational condition for the belief in revelation, the rational ground (*raison*) for the acceptance of revealed faith. At the same time it would solve the problem of the " point of insertion " for Christianity.[60] What has happened here calls for no further commentary. An epistemological question has been changed by Möhler into a metaphysical one by taking the Bishop of Strasbourg's *par le raisonnement seul* as a " natural " faculty and broadening the question to make it concern " natural knowledge " in general.

By this, Möhler also made it possible for himself to expound what is to be understood by the natural man's existence before God. It is an interpretation in terms of a religious philosophy of our knowledge of God, taking as its basis the magnitude and the limits of the fall of man;[61] a philosophy springing from the natural rational belief in the divine image which has remained in man even after the fall, so that man still finds himself in possession of the capacity to know and will divine things.[62] In his early period down to his work on St. Anselm, Möhler had regarded all knowledge of God as deriving from the Gospel or the teaching of the Church (regarded as the Gospel in its living objective form). That was Bautain's view also. Now, however, Möhler holds there can be no question of dogma drawing *all* conviction of God's existence from the Gospel and grace or from Mosaic revelation as the case may be. After all, the fifth chapter of the Synod of Orange, A.D. 529, confirmed by the Apostolic See, clearly speaks in its conclusion of a natural belief in God outside the Church.[63] The synod throughout assumes that man of himself can have a rational belief in God and his attributes.[64] In the *Einheit,* Möhler had rejected a knowledge of God from the nature of man. There he took it as established that " without special revelation there is no knowledge of God ".[65] Now, however, he affirms " the possibility and reality of attaining a conviction of God's existence and attributes without special revelation and grace ".[66]

That a rational, natural belief or faith is possible to man left to himself has its basis, he thinks, in the fact that dogma attributes to fallen man freedom of choice, *liberum arbitrium,* even if only in a weakened form. Now this concerns both the cognitive and volitional faculties. So Möhler's interpretation of the concrete situation of man before God as determined by the magnitude and limits of the fall has its starting point in natural man as a whole. But even in the fundamental part of his interpretation, which concerns the philosophy of religion, Möhler places moral freedom in the centre. We can therefore identify as a principle of this defence of faith, in view of its dogmatic basis, the affirmation that it is always the whole man who stands before God. No knowledge of God, and consequently no natural knowledge of God, is a necessary knowledge; it is always morally determined, that is to say, free knowledge and recognition, voluntary consent to and affirmation of God's existence and the infinite perfection of his attributes, in other words, rational faith.[67] But what exactly is meant by this?

Knowledge of God is a direct knowledge and a morally conditioned affirmation of this knowledge. That is what Möhler means by the rational faith of the whole natural man. In the basis which he assigns to this faith, however, his anti-rationalist attitude makes its presence felt. From the start he dismisses all individualism from his interpretation of the concrete situation of the natural man in relation to God. This is where Möhler's Traditionalism comes in. The question of the knowledge of God by natural man would, he thinks, present no meaning if what were postulated were an individual human reason absolutely in itself. For there is no human being left to himself to that extent, as a general rule. By his very nature man lives in the company of his kind. Consequently, for man the knowledge of God is ultimately a moral problem and therefore one of education. Religious development is bound up with the general laws of mental growth. A religious Robinson Crusoe is an absurdity. There is never any knowledge of God except in and through society. The autonomous individual, the human being left to himself, a person shut up from birth in a cave or a dark room, would never of himself attain a knowledge of God. Even a human being who was withdrawn from childhood from his human environment and placed in the animal world would not attain any use of reason and would not advance beyond the animal stage. It is only through education of human being by human being, through mental influence and the communication of spiritual values and their handing down that man achieves a really human life. The degree of his own mental culture corresponds to the level of culture around him. Even in free intercourse with nature or in a human environment that lacked any form of divine worship and never spoke of what is higher and divine, man would never come to a rational belief in God. This had already been maintained by Möhler's master, Drey.

For Möhler, therefore, the question of natural man's life in relation to God is " whether (fallen) man, viewed with all his powers and faculties in human society and with all the means of mental cultivation it offers, but without Mosaic or Christian revelation and without the grace of God operative within him is able to recognize and believe God's existence and attributes.' When it is asked whether the natural man can know about God, it is a question of considering " whether the human being, who is without the divine provisions just mentioned can, under the general guidance and help of divine providence make such a rational use of his physical and mental environment and of all the higher forces that may be at work in his age and also of his own inner world that he can attain the knowledge in question through his own reason ".[68]

The help of his mental environment implies that man's knowledge of God and of divine things must in some way be derived from that environment. For without the society of other human beings who already possess some knowledge in general and some religious knowledge in particular, a man would never reach the beginning of intellectual and religious development; he would live like an animal, despite his rational endowment, " without speech and without thought ".[69] Where the word " God " does not ring in the ears of men, they remain without thought of God. Here Möhler agrees with Bonald and Bautain.[70] In the religious philosophy of Bautain and Möhler, Jacobi's rational faith has united with the ideas of French Traditionalism. For Bautain's philosophy of faith, too, is undeniably inspired by Jacobi. This is obvious in a man who had such an excellent knowledge of German Idealism, and Möhler directly refers to the influence of Jacobi when he criticizes what Bautain has to say on the proofs of the existence of God.[71] Möhler also interprets the Pauline doctrine of the pagan's natural knowledge of God in a Traditionalist sense. When Paul says that man by the light of his reason, since the creation of the world, has known God's invisible nature, his eternal power and divinity (Rom 1 : 18-21), Möhler understands by " man ", not human nature in an abstract and theoretical way in the individual, but man in his actual concrete existence : " Man in society, as he actually and historically exists ".[72] For the Möhler of the letter to Bautain, that means man to whom the name " God " and, with the word " God ", the concept of God is conveyed by human society through tradition and who, believing, accepts this. But if this is the law according to which natural man approaches God, then in the very beginning, on the morning of creation, the word " God " must first have rung out for man to have had any thought of God. At the beginning of all knowledge of God, even that of natural man, stands the God who makes known his name, so that by tradition it may ring out from generation to generation in the human race. The word of God concerning himself becomes a piercing watchman's cry echoing everywhere, continuing to ring out in humanity so that sleeping reason may awake and recognize its Lord. All knowledge of natural (fallen) man regarding God's existence and attributes has its source and ground in this word of God uttered on the day of creation, that is to say, in primitive revelation. The fact that the word " God " is uttered in the human race at every epoch and that the thought of God always lives on " leads us to the assumption that all religious culture that exists among the various races of men derives from God's original revelation to the first human beings and cannot be explained without this ", so that no man living in society has been totally without contact with this original revelation.[73] This universal revelation must therefore be taken into account when we seek to inquire what man can know of God for himself, by the use of his own reason. Knowledge of God without Mosaic and Christian revelation is universally possible, " for the word which names God is everywhere found ".[74] Indeed the word for God is in the language of all nations, through most ancient tradition, the first that is spoken in every human ear.[75] The name of God, however, coming to men from without, would remain a mere noise if it did not find within man something that vibrated in harmony with it. That leads us to the *a priori* tendency towards God which is present in the nature of man. Möhler regards this as constituted by the innate idea of God rooted in the nature of man like a seed which needs external stimulus if it is to develop.[76] He also regards it as present in the *desiderium naturale* for God which for him is identical with the need for full union with God which has its ground in the intellectual nature of man. This tendency towards union is fundamentally genuinely religious, an inextinguishable sign of higher powers that survive even in fallen man. A completely wicked man would no longer feel any impulse towards association with God.[77]

We can now sum up what Möhler understands by the direct or immediate form of man's rational knowledge of God. It is the assent of man standing outside Old Testament and Christian revelation, but inside the mental domain of human society, to the word and thought of God coming to him from primitive revelation through tradition : a direct, rational faith of the Traditionalist kind. This is the view which Möhler had already expressed in his works on Anselm of Canterbury (1828) and Islam (1830), and it explains why he held that Bautain was right and not the Bishop of Strasbourg. This is what his philosophy of belief had in common with that of Bautain. But Möhler, unlike Bautain, distinguished this form of knowledge of God from the supernatural form gained from supernatural revelation and supernatural faith, and approached in this respect the Bishop of Strasbourg's view by completing the natural knowledge of God in the direct form of rational faith by the natural knowledge of God in the mediate form given by the proofs of God's existence.

Möhler differs from Bautain because in addition to direct belief in God, he accepts an indirect knowledge of God attained by rational proof. The question spontaneously arises what need there is of proofs of God's existence if prior to these we already believe in him by reason. The proofs of God's existence—it is certain from the start—can only have a place within the antecedent rational faith in God. The only question can be, what meaning these proofs can have within the framework of this rational belief. The latter gives them their significance and determines their nature. Rational faith gives us a direct knowledge of God, but it is a knowledge that belongs to fallen man, which means that it belongs to man who has fallen victim to doubt. Möhler knows the consequences for the knowledge of God which inevitably result from man's life having been shattered by sin, shattered in what belongs to the natural domain of human existence.

"Through the fall, direct self-evident certainty has disappeared; man must observe laboriously and pitiably his own innermost self and vigilantly examine whether the name 'God' coming to him from without finds any response in him, or whether it is not an empty noise." [78] The significance of the proof of God's existence and attributes, therefore, can only be to bring the direct knowledge of God, the certainty of which is no longer assured, to certainty by means of a mediate knowledge. For the nature of a proof is to lead to certainty. "A proof that cannot produce any certainty is in fact no proof; we must therefore either accept proofs and look to them to produce certainty, or reject both certainty as the end and proof as the means." [79]

It is from the standpoint of rational faith that the nature of these rational proofs is determined. Möhler describes them dialectically through two contrasts. It cannot be a question with them of simply " conveying scientifically what is already certain ",[80] nor can it be, as Jacobi and Bautain thought, a matter of deducing for the first time God's existence from the existence of the world in such a way that the knowledge of God's existence would actually be the outcome solely of this logical process of proof. It cannot be a case of " deduction of one existence from another, reduction of a truth to a higher truth." [81] Proving God by reason must rather always be understood in relation to the prior knowledge of God derived from natural faith. From that it follows, however, that " to prove here simply means to demonstrate the connection of truths which are already perfectly present to consciousness with others that are not yet present." [82] In our case that means that the name of God which man first hears spoken and accepts in faith has also to be spelt out from the creation; that is to say that God's existence has to be manifested through creation as well. To demonstrate God, therefore, simply means to prove God's existence, which is always antecedently a direct datum for us in rational faith, through the creation as well, and so subsequently to confirm the direct knowledge of God which is already present. " To confirm in that way the word of God which by ancient tradition is the first in the language of all nations and which reaches every human ear, that is what is meant by proving God's existence and infinite attributes." [83]

How is that possible? Precisely in this question a decisive change took place for Möhler himself. In his earlier work, the *Einheit,* he had denied the possibility of a rational proof of God's existence, because, with Jacobi, he had equated the

69

logical order with the ontological, that is to say, he was of the opinion that what is first in being is also logically first.[84] Now, however, as against Jacobi and Bautain, he emphasized the difference between the two orders and affirmed that something can logically be the ground of another even though ontologically it has its own ground in the latter; something dependent on another for its being can provide the logical ground by which the independent being can be demonstrated. Logical dependence in no way implies ontological dependence. In fact it is quite possible that truths by means of which we establish the certainty of another truth really presuppose the latter as their ontological condition. Applied to the present case, that means that there is no contradiction in establishing with certainty the truth " God " through truths regarding the order of creation which are more accessible to man although the existence of God is the condition of the existence of the creation.[85] From the human point of view the possibility of rational proof of the existence of God has its ground in the fact that man is the image of God even after the fall. However deeply man has fallen, he has not lost freedom and the divine likeness.[86] That means that man " is endowed with higher powers which of their very nature are directed towards God ", and he has not lost these even by the fall. And so for Möhler the demonstration of God's existence by reason becomes an expression of the magnitude and the limits of the fall of man. The fact that it is necessary for man to prove God's existence indicates that God's image in him is no longer the original one. If man had not fallen as God's image in its original, untarnished state, he would find God directly in himself. The living thought of God would always be present to him. All creatures would bring before him God's likeness in tones of joy. Consequently, for Möhler the fact that it is necessary to prove God is itself a terrible phenomenon, the most striking proof of the fall of humanity in Adam.[87] But that it is still possible to prove God's existence shows that God's image is not completely abolished in us. " To be obliged to prove that existence is a sign that the divine image in us is inexpressibly obscured; yet to be able to achieve the proof is a sign that it is not completely effaced or extinguished." [88]

In this way Möhler has described the natural knowledge which apart from revelation can still be had by man since the fall. It divides into the two forms of a direct knowledge of God by rational faith conveyed to him by tradition and an indirect knowledge through proofs. The former is the foundation of our natural knowledge of God, the latter its crown and conclusion. Both are intrinsically related to one another. The proof of God perfects the natural knowledge of God through rational faith by giving this faith the certainty which it lacks. It is only the two together which constitute the whole of our knowledge of God in the domain of nature. By relating in this way the proofs of God's existence to rational faith, Möhler resolved in a higher unity the antithesis of the *via antiqua* and the *via moderna* in the explanation of the grounds of faith. What was decisive for changing the strict Traditionalism of the early Möhler into the moderate opinion of the later was the fact that reason was no longer simply a receptive, passive organ, but also an active, creative one. Paul Schanz was later to follow him in this, which provided the transition from strict to moderate Traditionalism. But even in his *Symbolik* he had distinguished, though not separated, natural knowledge of God from supernatural. That was also Möhler's intention in his letter to Bautain. It is true that by the very fact of clearly delimiting the natural knowledge of God, Möhler created the possibility of distinguishing it from the supernatural knowledge of God. But it is only done in order ultimately to relate the two and to exhibit their unity in diversity.

Finally, not only has the relation of a rational faith to rational proof to be determined, but also the relation of this philosophical religious speculation to rational faith. Möhler regards this too as a mutual relation because of the connection between the principle of authority and that of reason. Each is valid in its own sphere, one in the domain of belief, the other in that of theoretical knowledge. The latter is based on the laws and regulative principles of intellectual nature and life which provide speculative reason with the firm ground and basis on which it moves. It is that reason in fact which grasps the necessity of a positive divine revelation and of authority. Consequently the insight that rational faith is necessary is, logically speaking, something that is derived from the laws of intellectual life. But for this speculation to be entered upon at all, a prior rational belief in God is needed. What is logically secondary comes first psychologically. It is precisely this that shows the Romantic element in Möhler's justification of religion. With Franz von Baader, Möhler overcomes the Cartesian principle of the ego and its self-consciousness. Like Baader he considers it just as absurd " to derive the knowledge of God and the knowledge of all other intellectual and non-intellectual beings from self-knowledge (self-consciousness), as to derive all love from self-love ".[89] The deepest reason why all speculation rests on belief is for Möhler the derivative character of self-awareness. Man as a being totally immersed in relationships does not come to himself (in self-knowledge) solely of himself, though he does not do so without his own activity.[90] Before anything can be derived from the phenomena of mental life, that life itself has to be awakened, formed and matured. And this is conditional on external instruction, authority, faith, in short, tradition.[91]

4. *Franz Anton Staudenmaier* (1800-1856)

F. A. Staudenmaier represents the Traditionalist view after the pattern of Drey and Möhler, for he too regards revelation as the form in which God educates the human race.[92] For him too as for Möhler, the mind of man is not a *tabula rasa* as it is for Aristotle and John Locke; rather it is endowed with a " sense " of, and longing for, the divine, but of itself is not able to develop this into a clear knowledge of God. For him as for Möhler, the autonomous rational man is an imaginary entity; a young child who falls among animals in the wilderness will remain on the animal level, without speech. Speech is the agent that awakens sleeping reason in man, he affirms with Bonald. But speech is an expression of reason, the instrument of rational communication. " There is speech only where there is reason ", and it is the medium of education. It is through education that we have all attained reason. This is not only the case as regards the education of the individual by the individual, but also as regards the nation as a whole. The intellectual and cultural life of a nation is only possible through education which conveys spiritual values by means of speech and hands them down. Reason does not characterize solely the isolated individual but the whole of mankind. When communication and transmission is taking place, we have tradition. It is consequently possible to say that speech, and therefore spiritual and cultural life, only exist through tradition. But education and tradition can only transmit spiritual values that are already known. What is the origin of these? Where did the first human being get them? Surely only because speech and spiritual values were communicated to him, and this can only have been done by God. God spoke to the first human beings and so awakened speech, and with speech, reason, in those addressed. The intellectual life and speech communicated in this original revelation became a mediating principle and a form of education. " Just as God, the supreme being, is only known through his Word, the expression and image of his nature, so too man, a finite spirit, is only known through his language, the expression of his mind." [93]

5. *John Henry Newman* (1801-1890)

Newman, too, admits a tradition of the nations which goes back to a primitive revelation. According to him, the relation of the peoples to God is not limited to the organ of conscience, the power of reason and the traces of the presence of God in creation. For him it is " even very doubtful whether the phenomena of the visible world would of themselves have brought us to a knowledge of the Creator ".[94] In all ages there has been, and still is, a tradition of religious truths among men, and there is probably no nation without traditions. But where there is tradition there is revelation behind it, so that revelation is just as universal and ancient as tradition. Consequently it is from primitive revelation that those national traditions spring, " those endemic traditions that have their first origin in a paradisiacal illumination ";[95] here " endemic " signifies " among (specified) people, in (specified) country ".[96]

Newman also observes regarding the Old Testament revelation : " There never was a time when that revelation was not." [97] That revelation is equivalent to the natural religion which is " a tradition or communication granted to a people from above ".[98] To this doctrine commonly recognized by the pagans in many respects, there also correspond common forms of traditional customs and rites in the various communities, such as genuflection, removing the shoes, silence, prescribed clothing,[99] common fundamental rules, assemblies for divine service, an organized body with laws and officials, feast days and churches.[100] These common rules, laws and doctrines in the various national (endemic) streams of tradition are a confirmation of the single origin of all religious traditions from the one stream of tradition deriving from primitive revelation. These " scattered fragments of those original traditions " can serve as means of introduction into the Christian system,[101] and were points of insertion for the original apostolic kerygma (Acts 2: 14-36; 3:11-26; 7:1-53; 17:22-31).[102]

6. *Paul von Schanz* (1841-1905)

Finally Paul Schanz, continuing the line of thought of the later Möhler, professed a moderate Traditionalism, considering that it was its own best recommendation.[103] For " religion only offers the highest degree of certainty and the most powerful support of life if it announces that it derives from primitive revelation or is a power created by direct revelation ".[104] Thus for him the six-day week is a " remnant of an original revelation which Moses restored in its true light ".[105] Traditionalism mistrusted individual reason and thought that it had found the principle of philosophical certainty in a tradition going back to primitive revelation.[106] Schanz grounds Traditionalism on the contrary basis to that of the *religio mere naturalis:* " Without the ruins of a primitive revelation, it is not possible to explain the religious culture of civilized peoples. The principles of natural religion by themselves have never formed a real historical religion." [107] The religions themselves attribute their origin to revelation. Belief in a golden age of happiness and innocence at the beginning of mankind is one of the most definite and significant elements of the traditions common to the Aryans and the Semites. The remains of primitive revelation were sufficient for God to be known to some extent from creation by means of obscured natural reason, but they did not preserve men from numerous errors.[108] According to holy Scripture, God did not leave it to chance whether man would develop articulate speech and rational knowledge, but associated directly with man through speech. However the naïve and childlike mode of narration is interpreted, it is at all events to be gathered from Scripture that an influence was exercised on man analogous to what we regularly see between parents and children, teachers and pupils. The traditional element is so strongly represented in all education that to this day not a single exception has ever been demonstrated. The first man had not only to be formed in body, but had also to be mentally equipped with the use of reason and language and he also had to be given the stimulus to activity. Proof has still to be brought that man, if left to himself, would have been able gradually to invent speech and attain religious knowledge. Schanz quotes Staudenmaier's remark: " It is a strange thing to have a child told about its heavenly Father and then ask how the child came by its awareness of God." [109] So far Schanz is in agreement with strict Traditionalism, but he then diverges from it.

In contrast to extreme Traditionalism which viewed human reason as passively receptive, he regarded it as active, creative and capable of independent thought. The human mind of course needs external stimulus and support, but it is a human mind prior to these impressions, and its knowledge in content and character far surpasses what is conveyed by these impressions. Its reactions are of quite a different kind from the sense impressions. " The universal concept which it forms, the ideas with which it enriches itself, are so different in kind from what any particular perception presents to the mind that they can only be derived from the capacity of the mind for independent thought." [110] Consequently the basic principle of our intellectual life is: " What you have inherited from your ancestors, acquire, in order to possess it." And in fact we do inherit a rich bequest of mental achievements: " From the Aryans we have language, from the Hamites (Egyptians) handwriting, from the Phoenicians the alphabet, from the Babylonians chronology, from the Hindus the system of counting, from the Arabs numbers, from the Greeks and Romans classical culture, from the Church Christianity, and from theology religious learning." [111] We therefore draw on an incalculable capital of known and unknown labours of past history. The distinctive mark of human culture as opposed to animal psychology, which displays no development, is the possibility of advancing through historical tradition.[112] We treat the property that we have inherited as something that we take for granted without realizing what a tremendous outlay of spiritual and physical efforts these mental achievements cost our forefathers. But it is not sufficient, as extreme Traditionalism will have it, to receive and accept in a purely passive way what is handed down. Its fundamental mistake, according to Schanz, was to suppose as a consequence of regarding reason as purely passive and receptive, that with speech, ideas and concepts were also conveyed to us. The concepts and ideas conveyed to us by speech are not *ipso facto* our intellectual property. We must think them out ourselves, learn to understand them, acquire them in order to possess them. As well as the passive aspect of tradition, there is the active one of understanding, assimilation, deepening and elaboration.[113]

7. Conclusion

We have deliberately presented in some detail this survey of nineteenth century theology of original revelation. Joseph Pieper observes: " The concept of primitive revelation, which goes even further than Plato's saying about the knowledge that had come down to the ancients from a divine source, has always belonged to the stock of Christian theology. Yet it cannot really be said that the fundamental conception involved has had any particular importance in the theology of the schools. This is an objection that must be made to the average theological concept of tradition which is an arbitrarily narrow one; in contradiction to the real presuppositions of theology, it does not expressly include the sacred tradition founded on primitive revelation." [114] That may be true of " scholastic theology ", on which the present author refrains from commenting here, but not of modern theology in general. We have, I think, shown this.

Primitive revelation cannot, of course, be historically proved. Historians of religion can only observe that however far back they trace the phenomenon religion, it is a thing transmitted by tradition. When they reach the end beyond which they cannot advance for lack of historical material, they can only assume that prior to the earliest historically observable tradition there must have been another and yet another tradition, so that tradition is lost in limitless distance. The primitive monotheism which primitive revelation presupposes cannot therefore be established by the methods of the scientific history of religions.

In more recent times, of course, attempts have been made to produce historical proof of a primitive revelation. In the eighteenth century J. F. Lafitau thought he had found evidence of original monotheism in Red Indian religions and that this monotheism had subsequently changed to polytheism through sin and ignorance. [115] At the end of the nineteenth century the Scotsman Andrew Lang, inspired by the Romantics F. Creuzer and O. Müller and the missionary A. W. Howitt who had come across the belief in a Supreme Being among the aborigines of South-East Australia, regarded monotheism as the original form of religion and polytheism as its subsequent corruption. [116] Following him, the Austrian missionary W. Schmidt developed his theory of primitive monotheism and linked to it that of primitive revelation which he based on his investigations among pygmies and allied peoples. He tried to present the latter as representatives of " primitive cultures " [117] and they were subsequently investigated by the explorations of many other investigators such as Schebesta, Schumacher, Vanoverbergh, Gusinde. Schmidt himself worked out his theory of primitive monotheism and the course of the religious development of mankind in his comprehensive work : *Der Ursprung der Gottesidee* (12 vols, 1912-55), English translation, *The Origin and Growth of Religion : Facts and Theories* (8 vols, 1931). This theory, however, has been rejected by those who hold an evolutionary theory of religion and regard monotheism as the final stage of polytheism.[118] But such an evolutionary theory can itself be considered exploded. At all events Schmidt's theory has not been given so firm a basis that primitive monotheism and revelation can be regarded as well-established results of the scientific study of religion.[119]

Consequently nothing is left but to approach the question in other ways and to be content with more modest but well-founded conclusions. This can be done in the first place by describing religious tradition as a universal human phenomenon. In accordance with the theological principle that revelation presupposes human reason and grace human nature, we endeavour to provide a basis for the theology of the tradition of revelation through an analysis of tradition as a universal human phenomenon and to indicate from this the general structures and laws which also hold good for the tradition of revelation. On this basis we can then take up a position in regard to present day controversies about the tradition of revelation.

III

RELIGIOUS TRADITION AS A UNIVERSAL HUMAN PHENOMENON[1]

1. *A phenomenological view of religious tradition*

We are not concerned to describe tradition as a universal human problem but rather, by means of the phenomenology of religious tradition, to work out the general structural laws of tradition which also hold good for the tradition of Jewish and Christian revelation. For tradition is not confined to the domain of the revelation contained in the sacred history of redemption, the tradition of the people of Israel and Christianity. It is found in the domain of natural religion, as a universal human phenomenon. There is an essential link between religion and tradition, insofar as the latter is a manifestation of human social life. Religion owes its continuance to the fact that it is handed on from one generation to the next in its concrete forms, rites, myths and secret doctrines. If we are to determine the basis of the tradition of revelation, the forms in which it takes shape and the laws of its development, we must start with religion as a natural phenomenon. When different religions meet, it is a question of different traditions, whether they clash and their contrasts stand out, or whether the attempt is made to bring their traditions into harmony. But the deepest reason why religion and tradition are necessarily linked is that religion is a social matter. Wherever religion is in question, people meet, assemble, unite. Tribes and peoples gather at definite holy places, assemble at special shrines and at particular holy seasons. In all this they become aware of their own community. The Jews, or at least the pious Jews, went up every year to Jerusalem for the Easter festival, assembling there to celebrate the Passover. The early Christian communities met on the first day of the week, as the Roman governor Pliny reported to the emperor. Even in present day Christianity, ethnic unities still form living religious realities if they have a common shrine. Thus for instance the Alemanni who, besides their common dialect and certain common customs, still have their own place of pilgrimage and shrine in Maria Einsiedeln, and so remain conscious of their unity although politically they are divided into four parts, Upper Swabia and South Baden, Bavaria to the right of the Iller, Vorarlberg, Northern Switzerland and Alsace.

Since meeting and assembly is a prominent feature of religion, the sociology of religion has been tempted to see in this characteristic the sole source of religion, but this is clearly inadequate. It is certain however that the social side of religion is the well-spring of religious tradition. The social character of religion not only means that individual members meet and unite in order to carry out their worship and rites, but it also guarantees the survival and continuance of these during successive generations. For every social institution has its traditions which the young receive from the old and the latter entrust to the former for safe-keeping.

But there is no absolute uniformity in this. A time comes when certain forms of tradition are felt to be superseded, no longer up-to-date. Then they are unthinking traditions, empty husks like the carapaces of dead insects, shells which no longer harbour any living creatures. Traditions are always in danger of becoming soulless, dead and rigid, and are then simply a burden that has to be dragged along with difficulty. They are felt to be a downright lie by those who go through life with their eyes open.[2] That this does not have to be the case is ensured by tradition itself. For religious tradition does not remain unaffected by the state of civilization and culture of a people at any given time and this brings a new feature into its religious traditions. To the enduring element is added change, advance, development. The cultural factors with their development and their continual proliferation in specialized forms make it possible for religion to give more precise shape to the various forms of religious experience. Every special form of civilization has one of the fundamental forms of religion corresponding to it, every synthesis in civilization a corresponding syncretism in religion.[3] Researches into the ethnology and phenomenology of primitive religions have demonstrated endurance and development to be the most striking features of religion, which indicates the importance of tradition, for it is a means of preservation.

So far, however, we have only touched on the outward forms in which religious tradition finds expression and have not yet penetrated its real core which is determined by experience of the " holy ". In religious tradition the presence of an order of realities is manifested which contrasts absolutely with the secular order of ordinary human relations and modes of

83

conduct. In it a different reality is encountered from that of daily life. This is the " holy " which is manifested in rites.

2. *The laws of religious tradition*

This leads us to the first law of religious tradition: there is no religious tradition without ritual; ritual is fundamental to it. The rites of the mystery religions make the basic event perceptible and operative by positing it as present, and make it possible for men to unite themselves with the mysteries. The purpose of ritual is to perfect man and make him experience the law of human existence in himself: " The cycle of death, life, generation, without which nothing of importance exists, unfolds before the congregation in symbol or reality." [4]

This gives the second law: there is no religious tradition without myths. In them the deeper sense of the rites and the meaning of the original event which they render really present is revealed. The word " myth " here must of course be understood in the sense it bears for specialists in comparative religion and must not be taken to imply a prior judgment regarding the objectivity or historical character of the event in question. These myths give expression to a view of the world corresponding to a particular mode of life and they place human beings in a definite perspective. It is characteristic of them to be handed down and received within the sharply defined domain of a group of worshippers whose religious attitude is shaped and expressed by them. That is why the rites of initiation are so important, for they are primarily intended to put the young men in possession of the myths. Knowledge of them imposes an obligation of strictest secrecy. The rite of initiation has the effect of incorporating the young men into the group of warriors so that they fulfil the conditions for acceptance and recognition by the men of the tribe. This mostly takes place through the communication of formulas, unalterable texts which the young men must learn by heart and retain, and of chants which must be repeated precisely as they were taught.

This leads to the third law of religious tradition: there is no tradition without fixed formulas. The transmission and reception of myths is based on sacred formulas usually conveyed from mouth to mouth. For there is nothing random in the use of the words by means of which the content of religious tradition is expressed. Its fixed unchanging form, which outlasts the epochs and the human witnesses who serve as its instruments, requires the formulas to be maintained unaltered. This raises the question, however, of the origins of these formulas and also of their authority. Why was the formula decided upon fixed exactly at precisely that particular moment? And why was it laid down that it must be transmitted in that way without any alteration? And what kind of authority was it that had the power not only to fix the formula word for word but also to impose the obligation of its transmission? Those are questions that must be put but which historians of religion find themselves in many cases unable to answer. Yet those questions concern the enigma of the connection on the one hand between tradition and language and on the other between tradition and authority.

This reveals the fourth law of religious tradition: there is no religion without authority. This problem preoccupied French Traditionalism, especially Louis de Bonald and Lamennais. Every tradition is transmitted in the form of language, and authority ensures that the transmission is perfect by both fixing and imposing the verbal expression. Without a language, fixed formulas, chants, poetic cosmogonies taught and learnt, there would in fact be no religious tradition. Language and tradition imply one another and produce one another; there is the tradition of a language and the language of tradition. It is the merit of French Traditionalism to have recognized and pointed this out. One can agree with the criticism passed on it by H. Holstein who considers that its error was to suppose that the connection between language and tradition must be traced back to the beginnings of man and derived from the initiative of a primitive revelation by which God taught man speech. Holstein rightly regards this as a confusion between everyday language and the mythical language of religious tradition. For common language is a necessity of social life, so that the child automatically assimilates the experience of the milieu in which it grows up and therefore the language of its parents and surroundings too. He asserts, however, that by the language conferred by primitive revelation what was meant was the freely established hieratic language of religious tradition, which is the vehicle of the experience of the holy and as a consequence possesses special characteristics which set it apart from the changes and pragmatism of daily life. But the religious language of primitive revelation cannot be equated with the " freely established hieratic language of religious tradition ". For in the view of Traditionalism, that language was clearly only concerned with conveying primary fundamental knowledge of God and divine things. And when Holstein further maintains that the origin of religious experience was confused with the subsequent expression of the experience transmitted, what he says is correct on the supposition that such an originating experience is possible in the first place, but proof of this has yet to be brought. At any rate for strict Traditionalism there is no such experience. Holstein rightly draws attention to the main weakness of strict Traditionalism when he speaks of its confusing the spontaneous knowledge of God, which has its starting point in created things, with an original revelation by God's authority which, as it were, spelt out the words of divine revelation to a man whose intellectual endowment was purely receptive. But it is doubtful whether the only possible alternative to a mankind with a purely receptive intellectual endowment is an active knowledge of God by means of created things, in other words, a purely empirical one. It is after all also possible that the mind of man is endowed with a spontaneous *a priori* idea of God as the *conditio sine qua non* of man's knowledge of God, an idea which by subsequent reflective knowledge of God from created things can be raised to constitute a proof of God's existence. And here religious and cultural tradition functions once more, for advancing knowledge of created things is handed down and the form of the proof of God's existence is consequently refined, and the advancing religious tradition sets out much more clearly and nobly the spontaneous idea of God. One thing at all events was made clear by Traditionalism: as far as human reason in the things of God is concerned, it is not the autonomous individual reason left to itself that is in question, but the general reason, common to all men. And so once again religion is seen as a social structure determined by religious tradition.

One factor that must not be overlooked in religious tradition is that religious formulas are handed down in the performance of ritual. If such a tradition is to become an inner possession, the experience of the " ancients ", that is, of those close to the original event, must be relived so that in this way there may be access to the original experience of the original event. This experience of the " ancients " is given in the accomplishment of the rites. This shows the essential connection between ritual, religious formulas and tradition; the latter assumes reality in the accomplishment of ritual. Moses says to the ancients of Israel: " And when you come to the land which the Lord will give you, as he has promised, you shall keep this service. And when your children say to you, ' What do you mean by this service?' you shall say, ' It is the sacrifice of the Lord's pass-over, for he passed over the houses of the people of Israel in Egypt, when he slew the Egyptians but spared our houses.' And the people bowed their heads and worshipped. Then the people of Israel went and did so; as the Lord had commanded Moses and Aaron, so they did " (Exod 12:25-28).

These rites are inherited from generation to generation and unfold in immutable ceremonies. In primitive communities their most prominent feature is fidelity. Those who accomplish the rites, the guides of the novices, are certainly more con-cerned with literal accuracy than with spiritual significance. Yet those who do accomplish the ritual are nevertheless con-cerned with the complete renewal which the rites bring about, the new mode of being which they produce or restore, and the initiates are to be brought to some kind of absolute beginning, a new birth. And so, above all, those who accom-plish the rites have to preserve with meticulous accuracy what the ancients did and repeat for the good of the young what was once done for them by the ancients. They have to hold firm to the actual material reality and this, of course, always threatens to sink to mere literalness and magical practices. If this occurs, tradition becomes routine and soulless formalism. Nevertheless the nature of the rites is to give expression to the tradition of the ancients, to transmit forms of expression that have come down from those close to the origins, and to practise them punctiliously as instructed. In many cases it will not be possible empirically to ascertain the origin of such tradition. Historians of religion frankly admit that the problem cannot be solved on their level, not only because documents are lacking, but because behind the sources of each tradition so far revealed by history there must also be an even earlier tradition beyond the reach of historical inquiry. What J. Goetz says about the idea of God can also be applied to religious traditions: the question at what historical moment this idea appeared among mankind loses all interest. The idea is found more or less clearly in all forms of civilization—a fact which is a datum of the very structure of man, at least so far as man's nature is not completely falsified by civilization. Any date that may be determined will depend on the idea one has about the moment when man became man.[5]

It is a decisive fact, then, that there was religious tradition the moment anthropoid became anthropos. On the empirical historical plane, however, the religious phenomenon cannot have an absolute beginning. "Whatever inductive theories and hypotheses may be made, the problem of absolute beginnings (of religion) is empirically insoluble. We can never say of the oldest human perspective that can be reached or

89

that ethnology is in a position to reconstruct that it is identical with original humanity. Similarly the prehistoric evidences, in which with some certainty we can find traces of early man's spiritual activity, will always leave an immense past of total darkness behind them." [6]

It is into this distant past, therefore, that all traces of religious tradition recede. It remains a merit of Bonald's school, that is, of Traditionalism, to have stressed the necessity of going back to the origins of mankind. In fact, however far we go, religious tradition is met with: " Before religious tradition there is religious tradition ",[7] that is to say, the tradition which prepared men's minds for the revelation of Judaism and Christianity so that the word of the living God might be received.

This leads to the fifth law of religious tradition: its forms and structures were incorporated into Jewish and Christian tradition, that is to say, into the tradition of revelation. These forms and structures provide as it were the material, the expressions and imagery by which the tradition of revelation is expressed. This tradition, that is to say, the Jewish tradition, into which Jesus who brought it to completion inscribed his message and the fullness of the revelation which he brought to the world, was founded, from the cultural and linguistic point of view, on the remotest traditions of the nations from among which Yahweh chose his people. The word of the Lord to Abraham was completely new. By this word what we call the revelation of the Covenant began. Yet in this word of the Lord that went forth to Abraham there echoed the language spoken in the valleys of the Near and Middle East where sacred history was to unfold. The language, images and even the number of the rites employed by the revelation of the patriarchs and of Moses were in a certain respect prior to it. The mode of life of those nations, their customs and habits, the religious myths which they handed down, were taken over by the word of God which was addressed to the people which was the subject of the Covenant. At the same time, however, they were purified and transformed. Similarly Christian revelation took over the cultural inheritance of peoples and lands in which it was preached and at the same time transformed this. An example is the biblical account of the Flood (Gen 6 and 7), in which various traditions are incorporated without being harmonized. In Abraham's native country of the two rivers there is an account of a flood in the Gilgamesh epic which has the greatest similarity to the Genesis account. The destructive inundation of the epic, however, has become in Genesis the deluge provoked by sin, for this flood came because God saw " that the wickedness of man was great in the earth and that every imagination of the thoughts of his heart was only evil continually " (Gen 6:5). Although Judaeo-Christian revelation was something entirely new, it nevertheless represents a religious tradition the origin of which is very precisely indicated in the Book of Genesis: Ur of the Chaldees, Abraham's city. In the hour in which the word of the Lord went forth to the man who was to be the ancestor of the people of God, something absolutely new occurred which, through the election of Abraham, prepared for Jesus Christ and announced his coming. With Jesus, however, yet another tradition began, introduced into the world by his apostles who were sent to announce the gospel of salvation in Christ—the apostolic tradition of the Church.

This tradition too with its origin and the " mighty works of God " (Acts 2 : 11), to which it owes its existence, was linked in its inner structure and its continuance to the ancient religious traditions descended from the immemorial past, which now served to support apostolic tradition by lending it their language and culture. It is true that apostolic tradition surpasses them and indeed renders them obsolete, yet it retained something of what they had contributed. For just as God prepared for the Christ by the history of the people from which Jesus was to be born, so, too, he prepared the history which was to begin with Abraham. He prepared for Abraham and the Covenant which he concluded with him through the religions of Chaldaea, Abraham's native country, where he grew up. For Abraham, the father of the believers, comprised in himself as head the religious traditions of mankind before him. Without his being aware of it, these gradually led him to the point where he was in a position to hear the call of God which was to make him the ancestor of Jesus Christ in whom God will " unite all things " (Eph 1 : 10). In this sense it can be said that Judaeo-Christian tradition, although so clearly delimited in time and history, reaches by its roots into the most distant, primitive and indeterminate tradition. But that is not the outcome of an automatic, necessary development, but a free action of God and his grace to us, preparing for the Messiah from the beginning of the human race, from the first stammers of a mankind which could not but be religious, and inscribing in advance the times and moments when God was to make known the eternal decree of his redemptive love.

Viewed in this way religious tradition is certainly more than a merely empirical link binding together the generations and causing the young to share in what their elders have made. It is the handing on of good news regarding a gracious intervention of God in the history of man. If religion is to be understood, attention must not be fixed only on its lower forms but must be turned to the successes, the higher forms of religious life. For example Judaeo-Christian tradition throws new light on the first and original event which is made present by the rites of religious tradition. For the Jews, too, the Passover ritual each year makes present the original event, the act of Yahweh setting his people free by leading it out of Egypt into the promised land. Tradition is therefore more than merely historical recollection of a great event of the past; it is that event itself rendered present in the joyful proclamation that divine election continues and endures in the ever new fidelity of him who has separated a people from among all the nations to be his own. The significance of religious tradition in general is seen from this evocation of living tradition in the ritual of every religion. It is the living link between the generations establishing a community between them and it brings powerfully effective religious rites into line with those that have preceded them. By going back into the past, tradition links successive generations with the original event which gives validity and significance to the rites. It is evident that continuity and actuality are the two poles around which religious tradition swings. The sixth law is, therefore, that religious tradition is determined by this pair of opposites.

Continuity determines religious tradition. From this point of view the initiation rites of primitive cultures are exceptionally instructive. From the purely formal point of view, they are determined from the start by custom and fixed by unchangeable patterns which are transmitted by responsible persons and tribal chiefs. Whether it is a question of the kind of separation of the adolescents who are cut off from the community and, sometimes symbolically, isolated from their mothers in the woods or in the bush, or whether it is a question of the time and duration of the separation or of the age of those who are to be initiated and admitted to the ritual or of the actual rites themselves with their mixture of instruction, ceremonial, proofs of bravery and tortures, tradition fixes all these points, arousing in those taking part the feeling of unalterable fixity going back to the most distant past. This strict framework established in its smallest details is the means by which the " mythical " tradition is inherited which reveals the religious secrets of the tribe to the candidate, who henceforward has to possess and guard them. When the initiation into the mysteries is complete, he is " one who knows " and will willingly preserve from any indiscretion the secret like a treasure entrusted to him. This discipline of the secret is found in one form or another in most religions and implies that the initiates are the bearers of truths which they cannot and may not communicate to others who are " outside ", and who " have not received the tradition ", a phenomenon which continues to be found in the Christian world in occult traditions.

It is noteworthy that the fundamental words concerning tradition, handing over or transmission, receiving and communicating, preserving, immediately suggest initiation rites. By their very nature and purpose they are a meeting of old and young, of the old who communicate and transmit a gnosis clothed in ritual and complicated formulas with the young who are to receive the secret and assume the obligation of preserving it faithfully and intact even at the cost of their lives. A continuity is established between the generations which ensures perpetuity and guarantees the preservation of the treasure. It is a burden in two senses, a weight which the older generation lays upon the shoulders of the younger and a responsibility which the latter assumes and which it is under the obligation of transmitting in its turn.

If the only point of view were that of preservation, however, an impoverishment of tradition would ensue. In any case that would be a very superficial view of initiation rites. A deeper grasp indicates that they display the manifold significance of tradition and reveal in particular its character of actuality. This means that the rites accomplish what they symbolize, the renewal and transformation of human existence. For tradition is not only the transmission of a legacy of knowledge; it gives access to a new mode of being. From the interest that primitive men show in initiation, we can see that the true and spiritual man is not the result of a natural process. The real human being is " created " by the old teachers on the model revealed by divine beings and contained in the myths. They, the elders, are the élite of early societies. As those who know, they are familiar with the secrets of the spirit, the true human world. Their task is to make known to the new generation a profound sense of human existence and to help its members to take up their responsibility to be and remain real human beings and so share in civilization. As the latter for primitive communities consists of the sum total of values received from supernatural beings, the function of initiation consists of revealing to each new generation a world which opens out on things transcending the human world. That is what constitutes the actuality of tradition.

From this point of view tradition is not simply the reception of something conveyed at the end of a long line of intermediaries without there being any possibility of contact with the origins. It is rather a moving back, aimed at reaching the origins by eliminating time as it were, by a real and effective rendering present of the original, fundamental event, a real and effective meeting with it. This explains the importance of death rites in initiation; they suppress in a mystical way the empirical course of time, negate it in order to make access possible to the time of origins. In this way they represent access to life by passing through death. The essential event, which in metahistorical reality expresses the law of true existence and which is posited as present and operative by the ritual, makes it possible for this existence to be received and realized in his life by the initiate. This is the principle of his rebirth, for the initiate becomes contemporaneous with the original life-giving event. He is, as it were, taken into the original event through a symbolic death, in order in this way to be given life anew.

Viewed in this way tradition is the means of a total renewal, a rebirth. It is not only a burden assumed but also and above all an advancement. Through it a spiritual experience is shared in and this completes the traditional initiation and integrates it. As the final item of a long series, the initiation handed on coincides with the starting point. The man who receives the inheritance not only shares a benefit but is himself involved in the work. He has become an associate of those from whom he receives the bequest, a contemporary and emulator of the ancients. The deeper sense of tradition would be missed if it were only regarded as placing us in a position to reconnoitre a field long since worked over by the ancients. For it not only conveys knowledge but opens a way to the beginning and to new zeal at the start of the work allotted.

This interpretation of initiation traditions is an attempt to uncover by phenomenological analysis the deeper sense of a dimension which religious tradition opens out to us and to indicate what a universal contribution to religious experience it could make.

3. *The double aspect of tradition*

The works of G. Van der Leeuw, M. Eliade and H. Holstein, especially the investigation of initiation rites by M. Eliade, have revealed two features of tradition, receptivity and actuality. These studies view tradition as transmitting a body of knowledge from the ancients, from those nearer the origins, which is handed on for safe-keeping and is a burden laid on the shoulders of the young, obliging them to ensure that the religious capital acquired by earlier generations is not profaned and squandered. Tradition, however, has not merely a function of preserving but also an active purpose. For tradition in the form of rites, which place the initiate in direct contact with the original event, becomes for him the principle both of transformation and of rebirth. Thus tradition in its receptive aspect can be a stabilizing and conservative force and in its active aspect a factor of progress by impelling and summoning the *homo religiosus* to positive undertakings. That is the reason for the ambivalence of tradition which exactly reflects that of religion; for religion, as Henri Bergson puts it,[8] assumes a " closed " and an " open " form.

This distinction does not signify two separate kinds of religion different in content, but the two poles between which the religious attitude swings. They indicate the limits within which the tension of all personal religion is experienced and are not the characteristic antitheses of religions viewed purely objectively. By its ambivalence, however, the religious attitude shares in the dynamism of mental activity generally and is not something rigid which can be envisaged in itself without reference to change. That is a condition of its vitality. Tradition regarded in this ambivalent way is something capable both of progress and of regress. Personal religion must regularly clarify its impulse, directing itself towards the inaccessible God who is its goal, for it exists in the concrete in various modes determined by imagery and rites, that is to say, by the ways the holy is represented, and by the inescapable pressure of social forms, the family, the tribe, the social and cultural group, the Church. Paul says that the pagans can know God through the creation, that God has made himself known to them, so that their godlessness is inexcusable (Rom 1 : 18-20). He confirms this in his discourses at Lystra (Acts 14 : 15-18) and Athens (Acts 17 : 26, 27). The authentic religious attitude is a search for God and must lead to him.

But this search for the living God presupposes the purification and discipline of a just and upright heart vigilant not to stray from the right path. This is the dynamic aspect of religious life. Each time, however that this endeavour falters and this impulse swerves from its course, religious life weakens. Putting his own supposed advantages before God, man chooses the magic attitude of an illusory selfish impulse in preference to the authentic religious attitude. Magic is, therefore, a deformation of genuine religious sentiment within religious tradition, its antithesis and caricature, a degrading form of religion. Social pressure links up with magic, for its very nature tends to favour a religion of self-interest and conformity, of copying others; it turns against the powers that truly protect the tribe, the clan, the social order and the Church and offers the closed group the service of its tutelary divinities and " closed " religion.

Yves de Montcheuil in his analysis of the fundamental ambivalence of the holy, has described in a remarkable way the ambivalence of religious activity. As religion develops, it strives to focus the holy in a reality of a personal kind, in order to express in the various forms of belief and ritual a dependence on the divine in the proper sense, and aims at rejecting more and more the action of hidden impersonal powers, that is, magical ways of belief and action. For these corrupt the holy itself at the very moment when it is on the point of appearing. But self-will is promoted by magic, for in it men strive to obtain possession of formulas with which to fetter the divine. Magic disposes over the supposed hidden forces which penetrate the universe and by it man acquires their good will, turns their malignancy against his enemies, uses at will the power magic gives. That is also a proof that the authentic experience of the holy presupposes an as yet undefined intuition of a transcendent divine freedom which man can invoke and appeal to, but cannot bend and compel to his will. Hence the sinister contradiction at the heart of magic. It uses the holy and yet denies its significance; the divine that it exploits is both above man and beneath him. In contrast to this, religion as it becomes more profound clearly proclaims the dependence which the holy involves. For the ideal of absolute autonomy is quite opposed to the holy.[9] It is obvious that the ambivalence shown in men's attitude to the holy cannot be without effect upon tradition. The ambivalence of religion is matched by an ambivalence of religious tradition. This leads us to the inauthentic forms of religious tradition.

4. Religious tradition and conformity

Tradition in religion can become an element of immobility, rigidity and withdrawal into self-centredness and may succumb to the tendency towards " closed " religion. Conformity then demands gestures, formulas, modes of action which are those of the social milieu and in the extreme case nothing but the result of the pressures exercised by society. Such social pressure tends gradually to suppress every spontaneous personal impulse, threatens to reduce spiritual autonomy to a tenuous flicker, to regiment and to impose uniform attitudes of mind. Tradition is certainly an inescapable feature of social life and the normal expression of a genuine personal attitude, but in that way it is degraded into an aping of the crowd, a collective attitude. The collectivity, however, which is very skilful in exploiting tradition to its own advantage, likes to make tradition a rigid, conformist force, a support of the pressure the collectivity exerts. Moreover, that pressure has allies in men's sloth and self-interest. What is more comfortable and natural than docilely to follow custom? Viewed in this way, tradition is an economy of force, marked consideration for men's autonomy and a contribution to the maintenance of public order—to one's own advantage and profit. In this way the transition from habits of social conformity in the narrower sense to conformity in religion is greatly facilitated. For religious tradition, as a complex of attitudes, actions and rites imposed by custom, is a part of private and public traditions. If in addition a tradition is protected by the laws of the State, a breach can even be punished by death. In the Graeco-Roman city-states, as the case of Socrates shows, impiety was a capital crime. It is easy then for religious tradition to be put on the same level as social custom, and this inevitably degrades it into routine and social conformity. At the same time, however, this provokes the reaction and protest of genuinely religious persons and so promotes the genuine tradition.

5. *The genuine tradition*

There is nothing inevitable and necessary about authentic tradition. It is not so much a compulsion as a summons to rediscover the religious experience of those who have gone before us in its original spontaneity and freshness. There is no doubt that tradition comes to us by way of society; it is transmitted by family and education, taught by religious authority, a teaching authority. Its unifying function and cohesive strength are undeniable. But in that way genuine tradition becomes a personal summons, and only a personal answer by which men clearly express their inner adherence to what is announced to them can show in any given instance that tradition in the proper sense has been received.

6. *The ambivalence of tradition in its transmission*

The ambivalence of tradition is shown even in its transmission. The very words which set a historical tradition in motion from generation to generation are themselves ambivalent. To " transmit " may mean to make known a doctrine, to teach, to observe a rite, to hand on what has been announced in a precisely fixed form, to train people to act in a suitably practised way (not unlike putting into effect a police regulation). But to " hand on " may also mean to appeal to the inner consent of the heart and understanding, the inner adhesion of the mind, to an attitude which is a personal expression of conviction. And again, to " receive " can mean the purely passive acceptance of what one allows to flow over one because one cannot prevent it, but may also mean the spirited reception and personal assimilation of the gift of God. Yet there is no impassable gulf between mere conformity and genuine tradition and the corresponding attitudes. The one can lead to the other.

7. *The tension between conformist and genuine tradition*

Using Bergson's distinction between open and closed religion, we might talk of " closed " (conformist) and " open " (genuine) tradition. We have already indicated the differences between them. It would be an over-simplification, however, to present them as irreconcilable opposites divided by barriers. It is a question not of opposites without link but of an inner tension. For in fact in most cases the two forms of tradition combine in various proportions with one or other element predominating. And in any case it must be remembered that what is involved may be the whole religious behaviour of an individual or a society, which makes it impossible for us ultimately to judge this behaviour, of which God alone can gauge the sincerity. Considerable scope must also be conceded to the development of religious tradition in the family, which might be called a social development within the social structure. It is quite normal and in accordance with the nature of the family for a child to fit into living family tradition before he is in a position to make this perfectly his own in a fully personal way. At first sight this may appear simply as the pressure of the milieu, the family, which the unresisting child receives as the way imposed by his upbringing, his human and religious growth, until the moment comes in his intellectual and personal development when the adolescent perceives tradition as a personal summons. This is the moment which is so difficult for the educator, when religious education must proceed with great prudence and when a sensitive feeling for differences of age is needed and guidance adapted to the particular stage of mental growth.

But this does not happen only to the adolescent; it is repeated in the adult. It is quite normal for the pressure which every tradition at first exercises to continue to play a certain part in the religious life of the majority. But for the adult too it is not a question of freeing himself from a living belief, from conduct which expresses conviction and personal initiative, but of his achieving a conviction of his own and of accepting as a known and recognized obligation what in the first place was inherited, and so of actively incorporating himself into the life of the community. The path differs in different individuals. It may be short or it may be very long. Caution is needed here, avoidance of rash judgment above all. It must not be overlooked that God's grace is also involved, and this can wait until the harvest is ripe. God allows time, because he knows that the world of realities is much more complicated than we with our limited minds can even guess at. God can so ordain that his summons is at first heard only from without and may reserve it to himself, if the soul is truly receptive, to lead it gradually to personal conviction and interior life. For a tradition to which one conforms without being in a position to make it one's own inner conviction is far from being on that account a purely external compulsion, incapable of awakening a personal religious life. The way a man responds as the word of God becomes more insistent for him is ultimately the decisive factor in what personally concerns him. And that is interior, spiritual progress.

8. *The historical forms of religious tradition*

Phenomenology and sociology have displayed the essential structures of religious tradition. The new question which we have to put is that of its historical forms. We have already seen that research in the history of religions has not succeeded in historically determining the original historical form of religious tradition. In fact behind the oldest historical form yet discovered we have to postulate even older forms. We observed that there is religious tradition from the moment when man became man, when he evolved from man-like earlier forms into *homo sapiens*. With *homo sapiens* we have to take into account his religion and, consequently, tradition. Was it worship of the one God? There are some indications that it was, but nothing is certain. We must therefore be content to characterize the forms of religious tradition which have been historically established so far. G. Krüger has set out analytically the historical forms of traditions.

The metaphysical presupposition for tradition to exist at all is that there is one all-governing Being who appears inescapably to our understanding as being, by what he is, the ground on which the whole structure of the world in essence and existence depends; in short, the natural revelation of God in the works of his creation, which is the ground of man's enduring existence as man with his tradition. God gave this to man, entrusting and committing it to him for him to dominate it. It is what God "handed over to us" at the beginning of his creation: primitive tradition. And it would continue to endure if man in principle allowed the nature of things to speak on all levels, so that they appeared to him with absolutely binding religious force as an intrinsically ordered whole with a single all-governing origin, a divine *arche*.[10]

But in the world of man as it is, there is not only tradition, there is also history; it is even possible for all tradition, all that is firm and enduring, to perish, and for only what is mutable, history in other words, to remain. The reason is that by means of the freedom with which his Creator endowed him, man can form his own arbitrary conceptions of the world, and does so. The beginning of these self-formed arbitrary pictures of the world is historically lost to us in impenetrable darkness, because no historical sources survive to throw light on it. Their origin is also a philosophical enigma. They are connected with man's fall from God and the reason why man fell from God is wrapped in permanent darkness. Only certain forms of such arbitrary views of the world are accessible to us. They appear as mythical thought which puts in place of God the most striking powers in the world, such as fire (fire-worshippers), or as magical thought which considers it possible to bring the divine powers under control and strives to do so. The common link between the human beings involved is the idea of divine powers, and this link is the source of historical tradition. It is no longer the primitive tradition but its reshaping and distortion into the historical forms of magical or mythical tradition. Just as the divine powers dominate mankind by their superior might, so too these forms of tradition dominate man's personal individual freedom. Hence the archaic rigidity of these traditions in which the individual is aware of himself only as a member of the tribe or clan. But that is also the reason for their long life, which could only be overcome by a higher development of human civilization, giving man his personal freedom.

In the West this was achieved by the Greeks who discovered humanity in man and so inaugurated the age of humane culture. With this the tradition began which was to replace the mythical and magical traditions, the humane tradition of which the decisive factor was freedom. This freedom, however, may assume two forms, an arbitrary sovereign freedom, self-based, responsible to itself, or a religiously grounded freedom responsible to the divine and taking its direction from the essence of the world and its ultimate ground. The former is the concept of freedom of the Greek " Enlightenment " which in fact took the form of a very decided criticism of religion; the second is the conception of freedom of the representatives of metaphysical philosophy, Heraclitus, Parmenides, Socrates, Plato, Aristotle, whose thought culminated in the question of God. Common to both, however, was the fact that they derived from myth and also that they both raised the question of God and the world. That is also the reason why in the historical, that is to say, in the second historically ascertainable form of tradition, despite the mutability which history involves, the true primitive tradition remained alive, and human life did not break down completely, despite the upheavals of the struggle for truth, and that there was not only a revolution, but an armistice as well, and therefore permanence in the relatively stable epochs. The latter had an enduring and unchanging mode of life, relatively lasting social forms, which means that they were determined by tradition, not of course by primitive tradition in its purity but by a new reshaping of it, the historical tradition of their particular age.

What characterized the latter was the fact that it allowed personal freedom to exist, and even stimulated it. But as it was only capable of forming a merely relative picture of the world, personal freedom was obliged sooner or later to criticize that historically conditioned view and to urge its development and consequent alteration. That tradition resembled therefore a great river which does not always continue on its course but sometimes slows and spreads into a lake. But here too the moment comes when criticism opens breaches in the banks, and the waters flow. The lake once again becomes a river only to repeat the process later with the emergence of a new form of historical tradition. Change is thus the law of historical tradition. This historical form of tradition was truly a tradition, because in it a revolution in personal freedom achieved a certain equilibrium. But it was a tradition in which a new revolution was already preparing. It was a genuine form of tradition nevertheless because its representatives considered the world that formed its background as the real world itself. And that is a necessary presupposition for the existence of any tradition. The men of the historical tradition did not realize at all the merely relative character of their age and even less the relativity of a mere view of the world. And that was the case even down to modern times, as long as tradition was stronger than the Enlightenment, which fought against it. But the destruction of all tradition set in by the end of the eighteenth century with the Enlightenment.

The hour struck in which the view formed of the world was no longer regarded as genuine knowledge of the one, objective, real world taking its place in the tradition of knowledge. Historical tradition experienced, as we have observed, revolutions which overthrew an earlier historical tradition. But a new tradition took its place and people thought they had found the final truth in it. There was no complete break. Each new tradition had something in common with all previous traditions: the *one* real world. What happened in a newly-emerging tradition was simply that the previous view of the world had to submit to remodelling: " History was always simply a struggle for a correct understanding of tradition." [11]

This ceased when the world picture was replaced by arbitrary views of the world following one another in rapid succession, so bringing about the disintegration of the common humanity that linked them all. For previous tradition, despite all the changes which its view of the world had had to undergo, was always simply the continuation and reshaping of the preceding historical tradition, and to that extent genuine tradition. In all earlier changes, as compared with those of the present day, a good deal of tradition was preserved; this was so even down to the eighteenth-century Enlightenment: the mode of thought of Greek philosophy and science, a feeling for the art of antiquity, the concepts of Roman law, the ideal of civilized humanity. For even the Enlightenment took over quite a number of ideas from the traditional Christianity of the Church, above all Christian ethics. It was only with the discovery of history during the transition from the eighteenth to the nineteenth century that tradition completely lost its power. History now liberated itself from tradition and made itself independent; history took the place of tradition and, because free of it, became increasingly revolutionary and devoid of any generally recognized human content. The really existing world dissolved into purely subjective views of the world, so that in the end nothing objective would subsist and nihilism would be the final outcome, if modern man were rigorously logical. " If tradition were really wholly eliminated, nihilism would be complete. If there were nothing at all that still stood firm, there would no longer be any possibility whatever of appealing to fundamentals of our common humanity taken for granted as a matter of course." [12] Fortunately, however, " we still live, in fact, even today to a decisive extent in traditions—in the tradition of Romanticism, the tradition of the Enlightenment and despite all our modernity, in the older traditions of the ancient world and of Christianity ".[13]

As regards these older traditions, " it will always have to be recognized how Church and theology in the face of un-bridled individualism and enthusiasm for progress, where the individual is a law to himself, held firm to the human personality in relation to God and normative principles. To the freedom of the individual they opposed divine authority which marks its definitive limits. They never ceased to see the individual as a member of a society that existed before him and includes him, family, nation, State, Church. They opposed the onward thrust of the belief in progress with the counter-poise of the preservative and fostering function of custom and tradition, and held fast to the historical tradition of Platonism and Aristotelianism. Those were the basic ideas with which Church and theology justified and provided a basis for living tradition in the face of modern ideology ".[14]

9. *Conclusion*

The historical forms and the fate of religious tradition which they manifest suffer catastrophe, but on the other hand show the inextinguishable need man has of the support of tradition. Against this background, revealed religion has a quite different impact from what it has when it is presented in isolation. The phenomenology and sociology of religious tradition have also thrown light on the fundamental structures of the tradition of revelation and the significance of rites and the formulas linked to them, and have drawn attention to conformity and the revolt against it as structures found in revealed tradition as in others. That analysis has indicated a defect of our theology hitherto in regard to the tradition of revelation. It left out of account the subjective attitudes taken up towards that tradition. The ambivalence of tradition and of its transmission, the attitude of conformity or of non-conformity to tradition, have so far remained unknown quantities to it. In future it will no longer be possible to pass them by, and our theology of tradition will have to include an additional chapter on subjective attitudes towards tradition. Quite recently a Protestant dignitary drew attention to conformity as a concealed danger of modern church life. People have their children baptized and confirmed, have church weddings and funerals, but do not believe in a personal God. How far has the loss of religious substance, the new mode of life in the affluent society, the break-up of the family through mothers going out to work, destroyed its religious tradition and led to the conformist pattern of the one or two child family? Is attendance at divine worship still a duty felt as a personal one, or is it only a case of conforming? These are questions which affect the basis of our traditional church life and which cannot be ignored.

Religious tradition has also shown us that the secret knowledge transmitted in initiation rites with minute verbal precision over the generations, the living word of mythical tradition extending over millennia, was the first and only means of handing down tradition. There was also the fact that the religious formulas were conveyed in connection with the performance of the ritual which took place with unvarying ceremonies. The unvarying words themselves bore as it were the consecration which the unchanging ceremonies gave them. Writing was added only much later; it is always a subsequent means, supplementing the spoken word in tradition. The various forms of historical tradition present the notable phenomenon that they reproduce the original tradition only in a distorted form, in the form given it by man who had made himself independent of God. On the other hand, when God's second originating word went forth to the man Abraham, the father of all believers, the religious customs and habits and religious myths were assumed by it, purified of course and modified and incorporated into it. And Jesus' new message and its continued life in the tradition of the Church remained in contact with old religious traditions descending from remote antiquity. That has opened our eyes to aspects of tradition previously unknown to us or at least insufficiently taken into account. They place the tradition of revelation in a new light, showing its unsuspected wealth.

Despite all the features that the tradition of revelation has in common with human religious tradition in general, however, it is something completely new. It too, of course, is an historical tradition, but it eliminates the defect that marks all historical traditions. It alone is based on genuine human freedom, because that freedom, as bearer of tradition, is supported by the operation of the Holy Spirit and a teaching ministry endowed with the gift of infallibility. Alone among traditions, therefore, it is not a revolution that has reached an equilibrium; it puts an end to all revolutions. With it, revolution is replaced by development from the absolutely new historical beginning posited by Jesus Christ. Of Jesus Christ it is really true to say what a pope once said of himself: I am tradition.

NOTES

PART I

[1] The early Church of course knew of only one exception, the appearance of Christ to Paul on the way to Damascus. Besides, this was not an appearance of the Risen Christ such as the Twelve experienced, but of the Kyrios raised on high in heaven. Since then there have been no more apparitions of Christ, but only of the Mother of the Lord. It would be interesting to determine since what date she started to appear (at intervals), and to what persons, men, women or children, she appears. At all events the early and Patristic Church knew of no apparitions of that kind, which of course does not prejudge their genuineness.

[2] J. R. Geiselmann, *Jesus der Christus* (1951), pp. 53-56.

[3] G. Bornkamm, *Jesus von Nazareth,* p. 156, note 14, English translation, *Jesus of Nazareth* (1960).

[4] G. Bornkamm, ibid., note 15.

[5] Heinrich Schlier, *Wort Gottes* (1958), p. 58.

[6] Heinrich Schlier, ibid., p. 59.

[7] R. Bultmann, *Theology of the New Testament,* II (1955), p. 98. Cf. also Ernst Finke, " Die katholische Wahrheit im Neuen Testament " in *Katholische Reformation* (1958), p. 150.

[8] R. Bultmann, *Geschichte der synoptischen Tradition* ([3]1957), p. 61, English translation, *The History of the Synoptic Tradition* (1963).

[9] R. Aubert, *Le pontificat de Pie IX* (1952), p. 354. The background to this saying is as follows: The Dominican Cardinal Guidi, Archbishop of Bologna, defended in the general congregation of the First Vatican Council on June 18th the testimony the bishops bear to tradition and expressed the view that this testimony has to be taken into account in some form or other by the pope when he makes a decision *ex cathedra.*

Thereupon he was summoned to the pope, and in the course of his conversation with Pius IX he told the pope he had spoken up for the bishops as witnesses to tradition. The pope is then, according to Dupanloup's Diary (cf. Mourret, *Le Concile du Vatican*, 1919, p. 299), reported to have answered: "Witnesses to tradition? There is only *one* witness, myself" (Dom Cuthbert Butler, *The Vatican Council*, 1933). There is a kernel of historical truth in these reports, for they cannot be entirely invented. But if the saying was uttered in one of the two forms even approximately in that sense, it was certainly not with the assistance of the Holy Spirit. It may have been said impulsively. At all events Pius IX spoke in this instance as a theologically private person. Even in that case, however, it was scarcely the remark of a particularly enlightened dogmatic theologian.

[10] Sess. VII, *De sacramentis in genere, prooemium*, Denzinger 843a; Sess. XXIII, c. 1 and 3 *De sacramento ordinis*, Denzinger 957, 959; Sess. XXV, *De purgatorio*, Denzinger 983; Sess. XIII, *De ss. Eucharistiae sacramento*, c. 1: *maiores nostri omnes quotquot in vera Christi Ecclesia fuerunt . . . apertissime professi sunt;* cf. *contra universum Ecclesiae sensum*, Denzinger 874; c. 8, Denzinger 881; Sess. V, *De peccato originali,* can. 4, Denzinger 791; Sess. XIV, *De sacr. poenitentiae,* can. 3: *sicut Ecclesia semper intellexit,* Denzinger 913; c. 8: *confessionem omnium pecatorum . . . (non) esse traditionem humanam,* Denzinger 918; c. 8: *praeter divinam traditionem*; Sess. XIV, *De Sacramento extremae unctionis,* c. 1: *ex apostolica traditione per manus accepta Ecclesia didicit,* Denzinger 908; Sess. XXIV, *De sacramento matrimonii: universalis Ecclesiae traditio,* Denzinger 970; Sess. XXIII, *De sacramento ordinis,* c. 3: *Scripturae testimonio apostolica traditione et Patrum unanimi consensu perspicuum,* Denzinger 959. Cf. A. Michel, "Tradition" in *Dictionnaire de théologie catholique,* XV, 1311.

[11] *Acta Apostolicae Sedis* 46 (1954), 638.

[12] The *certum charisma veritatis* does not signify the gift of infallibility, belonging to the episcopate as a whole, as it is commonly taken to mean, but the gift of truth in its objective sense, revealed truth itself; Karl Müller, "Das charisma veritatis und der Episkopat bei Irenaeus" in *Zeitschrift für die neutestamentliche Wissenschaft* 23 (1924), pp. 216–22; Damian vanden Eynde, *Les Normes de l'enseignement chrétien* (1933), pp. 186–7.

[13] *Neue Beiträge zur Bildung der Geistlichen,* II (1911) Foreword, III; *Heiligtum der Menschheit* (1810), p. 203; J. R. Geiselmann, *Von lebendiger Religiosität zum Leben der Kirche* (1952), p. 201.

[14] *Neue Beiträge,* II, p. 215; J. R. Geiselmann, *Von lebendiger Religiosität,* p. 201.

[15] Cf. J. A. Jungmann in *Zeitschrift für katholische Theologie* 80 (1958), p. 330.

[16] *Histoire et dogme (La Quinzaine,* vol. 56, 1904), p. 437; Lucio da Veiga Coutinho, " Tradition et histoire dans la controverse moderniste ", *Analecta Gregoriana* 73 (1954), p. 139.

[17] D. Koster, *Volk Gottes im Wachstum des Glaubens* (1950), p. 69.

[18] *Symbolik,* I, Introduction and Text, edited by J. R. Geiselmann (1958) § 38, p. 413; II (1960), pp. 715–16.

[19] First translation based on the 4th edition of Möhler's *Symbolik,* 2 volumes (1836); second translation based on the 5th revised and amended edition of the *Symbolik* (1852).

[20] J. H. Newman, *On Consulting the Laity in Matters of Faith* (new ed. 1963). Cf. also Günter Biemer, *Überlieferung und Offenbarung* (1961), p. 133.

[21] *Acta Apostolicae Sedis* 46 (1954), 638.

[22] Ibid.

[23] C. Moeller, " Tradition et oecuménisme " in *Irenikon* 25 (1952), p. 369.

[24] That the sense of the faith comprises all members of the Church is affirmed by D. Koster too, but he seems to take the concept too widely by regarding the official teaching functions as also comprised in this sense of the faith.

[25] *Symbolik* I, p. 415.

[26] D. Koster, *Volk Gottes,* pp. 72, 82, 98–99.

[27] S. Dejaifve observes (" Bible, tradition, magistère " in *Nouvelle Revue Théologique,* 1956, p. 150): The whole Church contributes to the deeper understanding of the Christian message, each order according to its rank and function in the *corpus Christi.* In this elucidation of what is implicitly contained in revelation, the initiative is commonly not taken by the magisterium. What will eventually be a dogma is usually anticipated by the Christian people, that is to say, by the faithful, as is shown particularly clearly by mariological dogma from

Ephesus down to the bull *Munificentissimus;* it is then given its due proportions by the theologians who compare what is developing in this way with revelation as it is already known and verify its compatibility with this; it is then sanctioned by the magisterium in virtue of the charisma that empowers it to make an infallible decision. The magisterium listens to the Church and also to the voice of tradition recalled by theologians.

[28] *Chartular. Univ. Par.* edited by Denifle and Chatelain (1891), II, p. 433. Cf. D. Koster, *Volk Gottes,* p. 126.

[29] Cf. my article "Tradition" in *Fragen der Theologie heute* (1957), p. 107.

[30] P. A. Liégé, *Initiation Théologique* I (³1955), p. 23.

[31] J. A. Möhler, *Die Einheit in der Kirche,* edited by J. R. Geiselmann (1957) § 25 no. 5, p. 80.

[32] R. Bultmann, *Theology of the New Testament,* II (1955), p. 98.

[33] The term *paratheke* was taken from ancient law (Jewish and Hellenistic). Cf. Joseph Ranfl, *Der Ursprung des katholischen Traditionsprinzips* (1931), pp. 192–206, 299–303. Kittel's *Theologisches Wörterbuch* unfortunately does not list the term.

[34] O. Cullman, *Die Tradition* (1954), pp. 45 and 43. On this cf. also K. Barth, *Kirchliche Dogmatik* I, 1, pp. 109ff., English translation, *The Doctrine of the Word of God* (1949), and H. Diem, "Das Problem des Schriftkanons" in *Theologische Studien,* No. 32 (1951).

[35] This is also admitted by Cullmann, *Die Tradition* (1954), p. 45.

[36] Pius XII's Encyclical "Ad caeli Reginam", 18 Nov. 1954 (see note 11) calls the liturgy: *doctrinae a maioribus traditae veluti fidele speculum,* Acta Apostolicae Sedis 46 (1954), 631.

[37] *Contra adversarium legis et prophetarum,* 20, 39; *Patrologia Latina* 42, 626. Bernhard Brinkmann, "Inspiration und Kanonizität der Heiligen Schrift in ihrem Verhältnis zur Kirche" in *Scholastik* 33 (1958), p. 221.

[38] S. Dejaifve refers to Irenaeus *Adversus haereses* III, 4, 1: ed. Harvey, II, p. 15. In Clement of Alexandria at all events there is no sign of Scripture beginning to gain ground as alone valid because it is the written counterpart of apostolic paradosis. If for him, too, the Lord himself speaks in sacred Scripture through the prophets and apostles, and Scripture is the highest authority, paradosis nevertheless runs parallel

116

as a second source. Just as it is the Lord himself who speaks to us in Scripture, so too is he the fount of tradition, the real teacher through tradition. He taught the apostles. They handed on the tradition to teachers who transmitted the apostolic seed and who inherited the doctrine from father to son. Thus there is an uninterrupted chain of teachers receiving and conveying tradition from the apostles down to Clement. But the believer who receives and accepts this tradition from teachers, perpetuates it for his part too. Consequently, Scripture, tradition and Church form a self-contained whole. " Just as Scripture bears the *pneuma* which fills it entirely, so too this *pneuma* rules in tradition as well, which contains the same powers. Furthermore Scripture and tradition belong to the Church, the Mystical Body of Christ, both are the continuation of the *didaskalia* of the Lord in the domain of history. And so the individual stands in the living stream of history. And so the individual stands in the living stream of divine teaching which develops in every direction." So Walter Völker, *Der wahre Gnostiker nach Clemens Alexandrinus* (1952), pp. 360-1. Origen lays down the principle (*De principiis*, Praef. 1, 2): " Illa sola credenda est veritas quae in nullo ab ecclesiastica et apostolica traditione discrepat." Cf. *Nouvelle Revue Théologique* (1956), p. 150.

³⁹ *Symbolik*, I, Introduction and Text, edited by J. R. Geiselmann (1958) § 38, p. 413. For the view just expounded, Möhler refers to Irenaeus, *Adversus haereses*, III, c. 3.

⁴⁰ Cf. my book, *Jesus der Christus* (1951).

⁴¹ M. E. Boismard, " Constitué Fils de Dieu (Rom 1:4)" in *Revue biblique* 60 (1953), pp. 5-17; J. Giblet, " Evangelium " S. Pauli iuxta Rom. 1, 1-5 in *Collectanea Mechlinensia* 23 (1953), pp. 331-5; E. Schweizer, " Römer 1:3f. und der Gegensatz von Fleisch und Geist vor und bei Paulus " in *Evangelische Theologie* 15 (1955), pp. 363-71; the same author's *Erniedrigung und Erhöhung bei Jesus und seinen Nachfolgern* (1955); R. Schnackenburg, " Inspiration und Irrtumslosigkeit der Heiligen Schrift. Neues Testament " in *Fragen der Theologie heute* (1957), p. 157.

⁴² Cf. P. Gächter, *Petrus und seine Zeit* (1958), pp. 105-54.

⁴³ On Stephen's view of Christ, cf. my book *Jesus der Christus* (1951).

⁴⁴ Ibid. pp. 9-12. On the complicated problem of myth, cf. the excellent survey of H. Fries, " Mythos und Offenbarung " in *Fragen der Theologie heute* (1957), pp. 11-43.

[45] K. Rahner, *Inspiration in the Bible* (rev. ed. 1964), p. 58.

[46] B. Brinkmann's objection to Rahner's evaluation of Scripture: "In that case the Church in the period before the completion of the New Testament would still have been incomplete" (*Scholastik* 33, 1958, p. 212), loses its point when the coming into existence of the Church is viewed in this way.

[47] On the question of the Canon there are two opposed trends in Catholic theology at the present day. One postulates an explicit revelation of the extent of the Canon (A. Bea), the other only a revelation given implicitly with inspiration. Cf. on this B. Brinkmann, "Inspiration und Kanonizität der Heiligen Schrift in ihrem Verhältnis zur Kirche" in *Scholastik* 33 (1958), pp. 210-13.

[48] Josef Schmidt, *Das Evangelium nach Lukas, Regensburger Neues Testament* (²1951), pp. 25-26.

[49] A. Wikenhauser, *New Testament Introduction* (1958), pp. 393-4. If the epistle to the Laodiceans mentioned in Colossians 4:16 is not identical with Ephesians, it too is an example of an apostolic letter not taken into the Canon.

[50] Cf. the profound work by B. Brinkmann, "Inspiration und Kanonizität" (see note 47 above), p. 228.

[51] Ibid. p. 229.

[52] J. A. Möhler, *Symbolik* I, ed. Geiselmann, § 48, p. 438.

PART II

[1] G. Florowski, "Tradition" in *Weltkirchenlexikon* (1960), 1474.

[2] Now collected in *Freiheit und Weltverantwortung* (1958).

[3] G. Ebeling, *Die Geschichtlichkeit der Kirche und ihrer Verkündigung als theologisches Problem* (1954), p. 6.

[4] G. Krüger, *Die Geschichte im Denken der Gegenwart* (1947), p. 32; now in *Freiheit und Weltverantwortung*, p. 123.

[5] Joseph Pieper, *Über den Begriff der Tradition* (1958), p. 19.

[6] Plato, *Phaedrus*, 274c 1.

[7] *Die Geschichtlichkeit der Kirche und ihrer Verkündigung als theologisches Problem* (1954), p. 32.

[8] Ibid. p. 34.

[9] G. Krüger, *Geschichte und Tradition* (1948), pp. 11–12; now in *Freiheit und Weltverantwortung*. Krüger has insisted, by the antithesis of tradition and history, on the essential importance of the unchanging element in the course of history signified by tradition, something which "quite definitely belongs to the fundamental features of the idea of tradition" (J. Pieper, *Über den Begriff der Tradition*, p. 18).

[10] Cf. 1 Cor 15:3: "For I delivered to you what I also received." Cf. J. R. Geiselmann, *Jesus der Christus* (1951), p. 44.

[11] J. Pieper, *Über den Begriff der Tradition*, p. 19.

[12] Plato, *Phaedrus*, 274c 1.

[13] Cf. *episkopoi archaioi*; those meant are Pope Dionysius and Dionysius of Alexandria, Council of Ephesus 431, Mansi IV, 1183ff.

[14] J. Pieper, *Über den Begriff der Tradition*, p. 21.

[15] Plato, *Phaedrus*, 274c 1.

[16] Plato, *Laws*, 881a 2.

[17] J. Pieper, *Über den Begriff der Tradition*, p. 14.

[18] Plato, *Philebus*, 16c, 5–9.

[19] Cicero, *De legibus* 2, 27; J. Pieper, *Über den Begriff der Tradition*, pp. 22–23.

[20] So Pieper, ibid. p. 14.

[21] A. Rüstow, "Kulturtradition und Kulturkritik" in *Studium generale* 4 (1951), p. 309.

[22] J. Pieper, *Über den Begriff der Tradition*, pp. 29–30.

[23] G. F. Creuzer, *Symbolik und Mythologie der alten Völker* (1810–12).

[24] F. Geiger, "Die Katholische Kirche" in *Der Katholik* (1821), I, p. 302.

[25] Ibid. p. 308.

[26] Ibid.

[27] Ibid.

[28] Ibid.

[29] Published in J. R. Geiselmann, *Geist des Christentums und des Katholizismus* (1940), pp. 235–332.

[30] Ibid. p. 246.

[31] Ibid. p. 245.

[32] Ibid. p. 243.

[33] In the article: "Aphorismen über den Ursprung unserer Erkenntnisse

von Gott—ein Beitrag zur Entscheidung der neuesten Streitigkeiten über den Begriff der Offenbarung" in *Theologische Quartalschrift* (1826) pp. 237–84; Drey was the author of this article which appeared anonymously: S. Lösch, *Die Anfänge der Tübinger Theologischen Quartalschrift* (1938), p. 93.

[34] *Theologische Quartalschrift* (1826), p. 279.

[35] *Apologetik* p. 3.

[36] Ibid. p. 4.

[37] Ibid. p. 18.

[38] Ibid. pp. 21–22.

[39] Ibid. pp. 22–24.

[40] Ibid. p. 39.

[41] Ibid. p. 41.

[42] Ibid. p. 42.

[43] Critical edition by J. R. Geiselmann (1957).

[44] *Die Einheit,* p. 117.

[45] Ibid. p. 98.

[46] Ibid. p. 99.

[47] Ibid. p. 98.

[48] Ibid.

[49] Ibid. p. 99.

[50] Ibid.

[51] Ibid. p. 120.

[52] Ibid. p. 117.

[53] Ibid. pp. 120–1.

[54] Ibid. p. 98.

[55] The letter is to be found in *Theologische Quartalschrift* (1835), p. 421ff, in *Möhlers gesammelte Schriften und Aufsätze,* edited by Ignaz Döllinger, II (1840), pp. 141–64, and in *J. A. Möhler,* I, *Gesammelte Aktenstücke und Briefe,* edited by S. Lösch (1928), Nos. 229, 309–29.

[56] Cf. Denzinger 1622–7.

[57] J. F. M. Lepappe de Trèvern, *Avertissement sur l'enseignement de M. Bautain* (1834), p. 5.

[58] Letter in Döllinger, *Möhlers gesammelte Schriften,* II, p. 147.

[59] *Summa Theologica* I, 2, 2 c. 3.

[60] Döllinger, *Möhlers gesammelte Schriften,* II, p. 147.

[61] Ibid. p. 154.

[62] Ibid. p. 145.

[63] Ibid. p. 149.

[64] Ibid. p. 141.

[65] Möhler, *Die Einheit,* p. 117.

[66] Döllinger, *Möhlers gesammelte Schriften,* II, p. 153.

[67] Ibid.

[68] Ibid. pp. 147-8.

[69] Ibid. p. 146.

[70] Cf. *Theologische Quartalschrift* (1830), pp. 91-93.

[71] Döllinger, *Möhlers gesammelte Schriften,* II, p. 157; cf. J. Kuhn, *Über Glauben und Wissen* (1839), p. 100.

[72] Döllinger, *Möhlers gesammelte Schriften,* II, p. 151.

[73] Ibid. p. 147.

[74] Ibid. p. 161.

[75] Ibid. p. 154.

[76] Letter of 17.4.1830 in S. Lösch, *J. A. Möhler* I (1928), p. 359.

[77] *Symbolik,* edited by J. R. Geiselmann (1958), § 1, p. 62.

[78] Döllinger, *Möhlers gesammelte Schriften,* II, p. 153

[79] Ibid. p. 156.

[80] Ibid. p. 156.

[81] Ibid. p. 157.

[82] Ibid.

[83] Ibid. p. 154.

[84] Möhler, *Die Einheit,* pp. 117-18.

[85] Döllinger, *Möhlers gesammelte Schriften,* II, p. 157.

[86] *Symbolik* (1958), § 7, p. 123.

[87] Döllinger, *Möhlers gesammelte Schriften,* II, p. 183.

[88] Ibid. p. 154.

[89] *Theologische Quartalschrift* (1830), pp. 582-3; cf. Franz von Baader, *Vorlesungen über speculative Dogmatik* (1830), 7th lecture, *Collected Works,* vol. VIII, p. 231.

[90] *Theologische Quartalschrift* (1830), pp. 582-3.

[91] Ibid.

[92] Cf. J. S. von Drey, " Offenbarung ist Erziehung " in *Theologische Quartalschrift* (1826), p. 269.

[93] L. G. A. de Bonald, *Législation primitive.* Cf. P. Weindel, "Das

Verhältnis von Glauben und Wissen in der Theologie Fr. A. Staudenmaiers" in *Abhandlungen aus Ethik und Moral,* edited by F. Tillmann, vol. 14 (1940).

[94] *The Arians of the Fourth Century* (1833), p. 152.

[95] *An Essay in Aid of a Grammar of Assent* (1870), p. 408.

[96] *Concise Oxford Dictionary* (1952), p. 393.

[97] *Grammar of Assent,* p. 431.

[98] Ibid. p. 404.

[99] *Parochial and Plain Sermons,* vol. VIII (1843), p. 5.

[100] Ibid. V, pp. 171-5.

[101] *The Arians of the Fourth Century* (1833), p. 86.

[102] On the whole question, cf. G. Biemer, *Überlieferung und Offenbarung. Die Lehre von der Tradition nach John Henry Newman* (1961), pp. 150-1; 165-7; English translation in preparation.

[103] P. Schanz, *Über neue Versuche der Apologetik* (1897), p. 157.

[104] Ibid. p. 386.

[105] Ibid. p. 307.

[106] Ibid. p. 104.

[107] P. Schanz, *Apologie des Christentums,* I (^{2}1895), p. 119.

[108] Ibid. 124.

[109] F. A. Staudenmaier in *Theologische Quartalschrift* (1833), p. 503; P. Schanz, *Apologie des Christentums,* pp. 124-5.

[110] *Apologie des Christentums,* p. 129.

[111] Ibid.

[112] Schanz refers to Goethe, *Materialien zur Farbenlehre, Collected Works,* vol 34, p. 253.

[113] *Apologie des Christentums,* p. 130.

[114] J. Pieper, *Über den Begriff der Tradition* (1958), p. 30.

[115] J. F. Lafitau, *Moeurs des sauvages Amériquains comparées aux moeurs des premiers temps* (1724).

[116] A. Lang, *The Making of Religion* (1898).

[117] W. Schmidt, *Die Stellung der Pygmäenvölker in der Entwicklungsgeschichte der Menschheit* (1910).

[118] W. E. Mühlmann in *Religion in Geschichte und Gegenwart,* third edition, V, 1459-60.

[119] W. Holsten, ibid. 989-91.

PART III

[1] We are indebted especially in this analysis to H. Holstein, *La Tradition dans l'Eglise* (1960); G. van der Leeuw, *Religion in Essence and Manifestation* (1963).

[2] Cf. B. Snell, " Tradition und Geistesgeschichte " in *Studium Generale* 4 (1951), pp. 339-40.

[3] J. Goetz, "L'évolution de la religion" in *Histoire des religions,* edited by M. Brillant and R. Aigrain, V, pp. 346-53.

[4] J. Goetz, *La religion des préhistoriques et des primitifs,* Collection Je sais—je crois, No. 140, p. 106.

[5] Ibid. p. 3.

[6] H. de Lubac, "L'origine de la religion" in " Essai sur Dieu " in *L'homme et l'univers,* edited by J. Bivot de la Sandée (1950), p. 293.

[7] H. Duméry, *Critique et religion* (1957), p. 201.

[8] H. Bergson, *Les Deux Sources de la Morale et de la Religion* (1932); English translation, *The Two Sources of Morality and Religion* (1935).

[9] Y. de Montcheuil in *Apologétique,* edited by M. Nédoncelle and M. Brillant ([3]1948), pp. 29-30.

[10] G. Krüger, *Geschichte und Tradition* (1948), p. 25; now in *Freiheit und Weltverantwortung* (1958), pp. 90-91.

[11] Ibid. p. 94.

[12] G. Krüger, *Die Geschichte im Denken der Gegenwart* (1947); now in *Freiheit und Weltverantwortung* (1958), p. 123.

[13] Ibid. pp. 122-3.

[14] J. R. Geiselmann, " Die Tradition " in *Fragen der Theologie heute* (1957), p. 70.

#153 7230